We Walk Among
ANGELS

Devotional and Small Group Study Guide

MARY J. WAGNER

PRESS

DEDICATION

I want to dedicate this book to Lisa Clemons. She loves the Lord with all her heart. Lisa has a servant's heart which is the best kind. The Holy Ghost has led her to cross my path and I am forever grateful. She has been a trusted friend who is more like a sister. She has compassion for others that goes beyond most persons.

Whenever The Faith Sisters have any event, she is always there and can be counted on. She has taken on the position to help sort all the contributions we receive and has even donated one of her establishment rooms to store and sort. She is truly a woman of God and I am blessed to call her my friend.

My friend Glinda Weddle has not left my path on this walk to share God's love with others. I will be forever grateful. She loves with her whole heart and I am blessed to have her as a friend for the ages to come. Glinda, you inspire me to be a better woman and not give up on whatever the Lord sends me to accomplish. You are a blessing and have stuck with me through thick and thin. Thank you for being my friend.

ACKNOWLEDGMENTS

To My Husband: Thank **you** for understanding while I spent hours on the computer working on the book. Thank you for sharing your time. I know God sent you to be the love of my life.

To My Editor, *Pamela McLaughlin*: without her this project would not have been possible. I want to express what an anointed gift Pamela McLaughlin has and is willing to share with others. She is a woman that has touched my heart and motivated me to be a better woman and writer by her inspiring thoughts.

I first was introduced to Pamela through Xulon Press. She edited my first book, "On Fire for God," and helped to encourage me through that book.

Pamela is an amazing woman with unlimited talent and I have been comforted knowing God has sent her in my path. Pamela not only edited but implemented the inspiring studies that accompanied this book.

We decided to share pictures and the picture came with her and the dog in the gardens. What a delightful picture showing her love for God's amazing things He places in our lives.

Words do not expressed what a blessing Pamela has been and I am looking forward to working on the next project, whatever God places next in my life.

Pamela, your work is wonderful and you have truly been a joy to work with! I have been so blessed to have God send you in my life. I know you are my editor, but I cherish you as a friend and wish you the very best God has to offer. I want to thank you for using your anointed talent to inspire others with your gift of editing and so much more.

Photographic Professional: *Leo Sparrow*, who also happens to be my brother, always inspires me to make a difference in others' lives. He has always stuck behind me through thick and thin. You are a blessing Leo, thank you for believing in me and all the prayers you have spoken over me.

Xulon Press has been a blessing to work with on both "On Fire for God" and this project. They are always uplifting and if you have questions, they are there to make your day better! They are an awesome Christian group to work with. Xulon, I look forward to working with you on the next project.

Most of all I thank the *Lord* for sending His *Holy Spirit* to guide me through this book and my daily walk. I pray you are guided by the *Lord* as you read this book also.

TABLE OF CONTENTS

Preface. ix
Introduction: We Walk Among Angels x
Chapter 1:   Protecting Angels 15
Chapter 2:   Fire in the Hallway 19
Chapter 3:   Crazy Trip with Shrink 23
Chapter 4:   Angels Take Time 29
Chapter 5:   Guide Me Holy Spirit 35
Chapter 6:   Blessed Friends 41
Chapter 7:   God Rings 47
Chapter 8:   Complacency. 52
Chapter 9:   I'm Grateful 56
Chapter 10:   Hospital Apartment. 61
Chapter 11:   Michelle Annie 67
Chapter 12:   Speaking Blessings 73
Chapter 13:   Are We Like Grass? 79
Chapter 14:   Pumpkin Seed 83
Chapter 15:   Pigeons 87
Chapter 16:   Unlikely Events. 90
Chapter 17:   Watch God's Hand 96
Chapter 18:   Joy of the Word. 102
Chapter 19:   God's Love Introverted 105
Chapter 20:   Straighten Up 109
Chapter 21:   Time Flies By 116
Chapter 22:   Are You Too Busy? 121

Chapter 23:   Boundaries 126
Chapter 24:   The Covenant of Marriage 131
Chapter 25:   The Blessings of a Mom 137
Chapter 26:   God Brings Me a Mom 140
Chapter 27:   Broken Pieces 143
Chapter 28:   What Piece Are You? 148
Chapter 29:   Airlines and Angels................ 154
Conclusion: Watch for Angels.................. 165
Small Group Facilitator's Guide*.................. 169

* A Small Group Facilitator's Guide is provided at the end of this book for those who would like to use these short stories in their home fellowships or Bible studies.

PREFACE

I f you have picked up this book you are probably searching for the truth about God's angels and how they touch our lives. Through my life I have been blessed to know angels have touched my life. In my previous book, "On Fire for God," I shared my time in heaven with you and how the angels came back to comfort me, walk beside me, and guided me through tough times. My life has been an adventure with the Lord, and my last time in heaven the Lord instructed me to come back to become a faith builder. That is my hope for you, that you will see God's hand in your life also.

INTRODUCTION:
WE WALK AMONG ANGELS

On many occasions in the Bible it tells of where people came in contact with and spoke to the angels. We "walk among angels" is a statement that we hear often. Psalm 8:5 speaks of man and reveals that God has made man a little lower than the angels.

My time here on this earthly plain has led me through many valleys and over numerous mountains. In my walk I've been blessed to have been touched by these angels sent from on high. They come to bring us messages to help lead or guide our way. They even come to comfort us in times of pain when we need an answer from our Lord. Many times they will assist us if we ask. We have to ask ourselves, do we recognize they are angels? Sometimes I wonder how many angels are waiting around bored because we have not had the faith to ask for help.

This book is to help you understand how we have the ability to ask the Lord for angels to come and help us; the same as they did in the Old and the New Testaments. Let me inspire you to call on the angels to help when you have a need. I am thankful we serve an awesome God and that He sends His angels do His bidding.

Angels After the Fire

When I was eight years old, I was burned by a stove explosion and suffered third degree burns over the upper half of my body. I woke up in heaven as my family on earth gathered around me in the hospital emergency room. I was blessed by the sound of the angels singing; what a glorious sound. God chose to send me back to my family that day, but now there are mornings when I wake myself up singing as I hear the angels sing the same as when I was with them so many years ago. I always expect to wake up back in heaven, but I look around and realize I am not done with what God has sent me back to do or surely I would not still be here.

It is a strange feeling when I realize I am still in my bed. My husband will roll over and tell me to stop singing and go back to sleep. It delights me to know I have heard the angels sing and have joined in with their song even for just that short interlude. Someone told me once that when we sing glorifying God, ten thousand angels sing with us. Isn't that the best thought? *Ten thousand angels singing with you and me as we pour our hearts out to our God.*

When I was released from the hospital and allowed to go home after being so badly burned, I was visited by two angels who came to comfort me. I would ask my mother if I could go down to the creek to get away. The sound of the rushing water and the rustling of the trees reminded me of the Lord's voice and the angels singing. I longed to go back to Heaven. When I asked the Lord to allow me to come back to this world I didn't know I would have these horrid scars. My family couldn't bear to look at me, and to tell the truth, I had to throw pebbles in the water because I couldn't bear to look at me either. I had no face, no ears, no nose, no lips, and no hair. I looked like a walking raw hamburger, and the unbearable stench from the burns was a continual reminder of my condition with every breath I took.

My daily weeping prayer was for the Lord to take me back to Heaven with Him. I'd plead with Him and explain that if I knew I was going to be like this I wouldn't have asked to come back. How could He have let me come back and suffer this terrible fate? Day after day this was my prayer as I sat on the bank of the creek pitching pebbles in the water.

Finally, one day the light like I had seen in Heaven landed on me. As I looked behind me, I saw Heaven open and there stood two angels. They told me not to pray that prayer anymore. They had taken my tears before the Lord and He had heard my prayers. They told me that I was not always going to look this way and that God would use this tragedy for His glory.

I sat staring at them in the light that was brighter than the daylight outside. This light was the ultimate bright loving light from Heaven. It was so bright I could see it coming all the way through the sky, surrounding me and the angels. These wonderful messengers from Heaven had brought me words of comfort and declared a prophecy that came to pass later in my life. I wrote a song about it and now I'm writing books to help inspire others to glorify God even in their times of trouble.

Song: *A Little Country Girl*

Written by Mary Wagner
A normal country day
But she was in the way
As she checked the stove
And the fire burnt her and so
A little country girl only the age of eight
Is about to enter heaven's golden gates
A little country girl only the age of eight
Is about to enter heaven's golden gates.
Now there is no pain here
All is light and bright
I think I will stay

No more dark evening nights
She hears his prayer, looking down below
Her daddy's prayer, "Little girl, please don't go!"
She hears his cry and sees his pain
Asking God above, "May I stay little while?"
A little country girl only the age of eight
Is now at heaven's golden gates.

As quickly as they appeared, the angels and the light disappeared and I knew I had once again been touched by God. I never prayed that prayer again, and stopped throwing pebbles in the water because I knew I was not going to have this horrid looking creature staring back at me forever. Not to say I received my healing the next day or anything like that because I did not, but I have not had any surgery and I now have ears, a nose, lips, and a face. My scars have gone both inside and out. Through the years God has taken the pain from my wounds and healed me from the inside out. He was a merciful Lord to send the angels to comfort me in my time of distress.

Just as He has done for me so many times in my life, God will send His angels to comfort, protect, and guide you if you learn to watch and listen for them. God has also told us we can ask Him and He will send His angels to help in our times of need. May we learn to pray for God to open our eyes as Elisha did for his servant in 2 Kings 6:17.

And Elisha prayed, and said, "LORD, I pray thee, open his eyes, that he may see." And the LORD opened the eyes of the young man; and he saw: and, behold, the mountain was full of horses and chariots of fire round about Elisha.

Chapter 1

PROTECTING ANGELS

For he shall give his angels charge over thee, to keep thee in all thy ways. They shall bear thee up in their hands, lest thou dash thy foot against a stone. (Psalm 91:11-12)

Have you ever awakened from a sound sleep and knew someone had called your name out urgently? Who did you think was calling you? Ever wonder?

How many times have you thought, just for a moment, something could happen if you didn't move that broom, shovel, box, etc.?

How many times does something happen simply because we ignore that still small voice we think we might have heard?

I think the answer may be, many times. Let me give you some examples from my own life and from those that have crossed my path.

Fans Fly

I'm a hairdresser and one day several of the women were talking about the Holy Ghost speaking to us and angels helping us. One of the ladies said she didn't think that was available to all of God's people, just some of us, and not her. I went over the whole spiel explaining how the broom could be in the very same position as it was yesterday, but this day you think for a split second, "What if someone fell over that?" If you don't move it even though you've been "warned," and then someone comes along and does fall over it; hopefully not hurting anyone, couldn't that have been an angel or the Holy Ghost speaking to you?

She still thought that it was just silliness. So I told her I was going to pray that God would send His angels to show her that this was real and available to everyone including her. That week went by and I felt I'd better call and check on someone where she worked, so I called and asked how everyone was doing. She explained all were fine, and then she shrilly started telling me about what had happened the night before.

She had crawled into bed and thought for a split second that the fan was directly above their bed and if the fan came loose it would fall right on the bed with them.

Then she laughed and thought, "That's silly, like that thing Mary was talking about."

I asked her if she told her husband to check the fan, and her reply was, "No."

They went to bed that night and in the middle of the night she got up to use the restroom and one of the fan blades fell off and hit her in the head!

"So then," I replied, "God had to literally hit you in the head with a fan blade to make you understand you have the Holy Ghost and angels watching over you?"

She laughed and joyfully said, "I suppose so!"

Don't let the fan blades or something worse hit you in the head. Realize God will send His angels and guide you by the Holy Spirit to help keep you or others around you safe.

Watch Your Words

I was explaining to a friend that we can make things happen in this world simply by speaking it out. I pointed out how God created the world by speaking it into order. Jesus calmed the seas and storms by His command (speaking). He even healed by speaking and brought the dead to life simply by calling Lazarus from the tomb.

At the time of our discussion, this friend was wondering why everything she was trying to do was turning out opposite of what she had intended. I challenged her to change the way she was speaking and let the Lord send His angels out in advance for her instead of blocking His help with her words.

She laughed and told me, "Oh, sure, it makes a difference what I speak!"

Then she said in jest, "I might even have four flat tires today!"

I felt like I needed to hold my breath because I could feel something was about to change her world.

Later that day I received an urgent call from her explaining her day of dilemmas. She had loaded her three children in the minivan and was off running errands for the day. As she turned into the gas station, laughing and joking about our conversation, all four tires went flat. The attendant came out to help and she asked him to check the tires as he filled up the gas tank. She said she was then very surprised by his strange behavior. He hurried as quickly as he could, put air in her tires, refused to accept money for the gas, and told her to leave as quickly as possible.

As she was explaining what happened that day, she was still shaken. She knew the angels came and let the air out of her tires because when the attendant filled them, they all stayed up.

"God touched me," she said, "to remind me He was listening and to watch what I put in to order with my words."

For years now she has spoken angels around her car to protect her and the others with her every time she drives anywhere. I'm with her, I do also.

Thoughts to Ponder

Is it possible you have been touched by an angel? Think of a time when you felt you had a warning just before something happened. Could it have been an angel guiding you, helping you or protecting you?

Stop and think today about the words you speak. Remember what the Bible says about the power of our tongues, "Death and life are in the power of the tongue: and they that love it shall eat the fruit thereof" (Proverbs 18:21).

Why not pray and ask God to open your eyes to see as Elisha prayed for his servant in their time of need and to help you guard your words. *"Lord, I pray open my eyes that I might see and my ears that I might hear Your still small voice, and help me to choose my words wisely today."*

Chapter 2

FIRE IN THE HALLWAY

Walnut Corners was a place of many new challenges. It was the first time our family had reunited after Mother had been so ill from a Grand Mall Seizure. We had been placed in foster homes until they finally located our maternal grandparents and we moved into their home.

This old home we lived in had a wood burning stove, but much of our cooking was done in a Dutch oven next to the fireplace. It made the best cobblers and pies you would ever put in your mouth. We did have electricity but only the lights were run with it, not any of our heating.

Our bedrooms were upstairs. My sister and I shared one. Dad and mom's bedroom was across the hall, and our brothers were down the hall. We had little kerosene heaters that heated our rooms, just enough to keep the frost off the pumpkin as they say. When they were lit they made figures dance like a ballet on the ceiling and we would fall to sleep watching the light flicker.

One night I had a dream that my dad was wearing a red and blue plaid shirt. In the dream, Dad was on his way to bed and had taken off his shirt as he walked down the hallway to their room. As he walked into their bedroom, the light bulb in the hall between their room and ours burst and flames shot down the ceiling and wall. I awoke startled and the dream wouldn't leave me.

The next morning I proceeded to tell Mom and Dad what I had dreamed. They did not seem unduly concerned. Whenever Dad would wear that red and blue colored shirt I'd always ask him not to wear it as it reminded me of my dream. "What if," I would say, "Why take a chance?" Dad told me that was ridiculous and it couldn't happen. He tried to explain to me how electricity worked and that if a bulb exploded it wouldn't happen like in my dream. I heard what he was saying but that ominous feeling still clung to me, I just couldn't shake it. The dream had seemed too real.

Several nights in a row the same dream would occur, and when morning came I would tell my parents again. Finally, my dad told me to stop that kind of talk because it was not going to happen. I really didn't believe him at this point because I was convinced it was a vision. I kept having the exact same reoccurring dream with the red and blue plaid shirt, the sound of the light bulb exploding, and the fire.

One evening after a couple weeks of this dream invading my rest, it was bedtime again. I had started to hate going to bed because I knew what I was going to dream, and I would always wake up fearful. This is one of the days Dad had worn that shirt I always begged him not to wear. As I climbed into bed, I kept saying to myself, "Don't let the light break!" My sister tried to console me and told me it was alright and to just go to sleep.

I felt like my teeth were on edge as I could see Dad taking off his red and blue plaid shirt in the hall and head for their bedroom. As soon as he had left the hall I heard the breaking of the light bulb the same as I had heard in my dreams over and over again. I recognized it immediately, screamed, and ran for the hall. Dad ran out into the hall and tried to put out the fire that had started running down the ceiling with his red and blue plaid shirt! My dream had come true just as I had seen it so many times in my dreams.

When Dad had the fire put out he turned to me. Of course I was babbling from all the excitement. He told me it was over and we were not to talk about it anymore! I think he was as shaken as I was that my dream came true, but being a parent it was his way of trying to settle me down and not think about it anymore.

I have thought of this many times and have come to realize we all have these experiences in our lives, if we actually thought carefully about them. Most people don't want to think or talk about what they feel others would consider "not normal," but I think with God this is normal. God talks all through the Bible of His children having dreams and visions that He has sent to warn them. The Bible also says God never changes. He is the same yesterday, today, and forever (Hebrews 13:8). Why would this change? We can pray for these situations or place angels around them to help protect those involved. We can even try to ignore them and go on without any intervention, but I personally don't think that's a great idea. If God sends us the dream or vision to help, we should accept it and be blessed that we are not in harm's way.

Thoughts to Ponder

We all have these experiences in our lives, if we actually thought carefully about them. Think back to a time when you either had a reoccurring dream or vision.

Did it actually happen? Why not begin writing these dreams down, track them through your journal, and begin to see just how many times God has sent warnings of what was to come. Take the time to thank God right now for the many different ways He works to protect you.

Father God, teach me how to pray in accordance with what You are showing me. Thank You that You never change and that You are the same today, tomorrow, and forever.

Chapter 3

CRAZY TRIP WITH SHRINK

There was a time when I was raising my children by myself; a young divorced woman with two children. I was training horses full time in Illinois. I was traveling back from an out of state horse show. I'd had a tough week and had hoped to have an uneventful trip back with time alone, a quiet reflection time. I had been running at a nearly overwhelming pace with the children, a full stable of around one hundred head to look after, and a training barn of about thirty horses to prepare to show. I was definitely ready for a break.

It seemed as if every minute of my time was taken up, but I must admit I kind of liked it because I didn't have to think about how my life was in such a mess. Having two children and being divorced by the time I was eighteen was not something most people actually try to place on their "to do list." I loved my children and wouldn't trade them for anything in the world. I am very blessed by my children and they are two of the awesome blessings God has placed in my life. Yet most people at my age were just thinking about getting serious, not thinking about raising children on their own.

So on my flight back from the out of state horse show, I had my seat arranged where only one other person had a seat next to me. I was actually hoping that no one would want that seat, but as it usually goes when you are in a confined area, not only did someone take that seat, he was a Psychiatrist. Even though I tried not to speak to the gentleman, he seemed determined to talk to me. I was trying to make it clear that I was engrossed in a book so I didn't have to deal with anyone. It had been a hard week and I was tired.

At this time in my life I wasn't what one would call a social butterfly. As a matter of fact, I was down right blunt hoping that it would offend people and keep them away from me. The horses didn't expect anything from me but care and feeding, that was something I could handle. I just wanted to do my job, hang out with my children, and work with the horses. They were both great company, and I felt I didn't need all the rest of the silliness that goes on when you are involved in other people's lives and them in yours.

This shrink kept trying to get me to talk about my job and all the other things in my life that were **none of his business**. I returned the questions with other questions hoping he would understand I was not happy about his incisive inquires. I know it had to be the Lord that sent that man to me that day because no man would want to put up with the way I was trying to discourage him. At least they would have gotten the idea and left me alone, but that was not the way it worked. Here I am with this insistent man who constantly is looking at me whether I am looking away and trying to ignore him or not. I could feel his eyes on me. Boy, did that bug me!

"What's the deal?" I thought to myself, "I really am going to have to talk to this man whether I like it or not. I just know he is going to try to use me as a subject and I am not happy with that."

I finally placed my book on my lap and thought, "Okay God, what in the world do You want me to do about this man You've placed next to me? It has to be you, Lord, because he is so insistent. No human is crazy enough to keep trying to talk to me when I am so obviously not interested. Since You haven't given me a choice and I am stuck next to him for two and a half hours, what do You want from me? Why can't I just have a little quiet break, Lord?"

I am sure more thoughts ran through my head of why I needed this time of rest and why it was unreasonable for me to have to deal with this right at this time in my life. Isn't it amazing how many thoughts can run through our brains in just a couple minutes when we don't want to deal with life's issues? I'm sure I am not the only one God sends these things to that we initially respond to by trying to argue with the Lord and talk Him out of whatever it is He is directing us to. Of course it's to no avail, He always wins.

Resigned to the fact I was not getting out of this, I answered his question about what I did for a living. I tried to take plenty of time and detail exactly what I did as I trained the horses. Once I got started I talked about everything from halter training to saddling to sacking out so the horses weren't afraid of objects coming at them or on them. I rambled on about training to ride western, English, halter, and driving. He would ask a question here and there about it, but I guess I knew I was just trying to kill time as they say, before he asked the probing questions I anticipated were destined to come.

Isn't that a terrible saying, killing time? We should be excited about every minute we have no matter what we are doing instead of saying we are just killing time. I didn't feel like that was what I was doing at the time, though. Truth is I just wanted the flight over so he would stop talking to me and stop asking me questions that did not concern him in anyway, at least as far as I was concerned. When I just couldn't think of anything else to tell him about the horses, he still had about an hour to talk, and talk he did.

He asked me, "How long have you been hiding behind the horses so you don't have to think about life and what you need to do to get it under way?"

I promptly told him, "I enjoy doing what I do with the horses and I am not hiding behind them."

However, secretly I started wondering if I really was. Sometimes it's hard to look closely at one's self.

He told me, "You can run but the problem will still be there when you decide to stop and take a look."

Ouch! Why couldn't he just be quiet and mind his own business? No one else in my life talked to me about my issues so why in the world should he? That was exactly why God had sent him to sit next to me in a place where I could not escape the questions that had to be asked. It was time to stop and take a look at my life. I needed to ask myself if this was what I really wanted from life. I had never really thought about where my life would be when I reached this age.

During my troubled childhood, I didn't think I would make it to sixteen. When I was married and had my first child at sixteen I thought, "I'm going to make it to eighteen." By the time I was eighteen and had my second child, I began to think I was going to live to be a ripe old age. Raising my children, making sure they made it through school, and seeing that they knew the Lord were really my only goals in life. Did I hide behind the horses, absolutely! I had done it all my life.

It started when I was burned badly when I was eight years old, died, and went to be with the Lord. I'd heard my Daddy's voice, saw my Daddy praying to God asking for Him to leave me on earth, and not to take his baby girl away from him. I asked the Lord to send me back to my Daddy. However, once I realized that meant many painful weeks in the burn unit and leaving the hospital without a face, I began to wish I had never made that request of God. I couldn't even bear to see my reflection in the water of the creek where I went to hide from the rest of the world. That was when I realized the horses didn't care what I looked like. As long as I was compassionate to them, groomed and cared for them, they were always happy to see me and I them. It was an unconditional trade I had grown accustomed to and it worked well. More of this story is in my book, "On Fire for God."

As this doctor and I left the plane, I often wondered if God had sent me an angel to get me back on track in life. The doctor's questions made me think about my life. God intervened in my life that day as I traveled back from a hectic weekend at the horse show. He sent this man or angel to sit by my side to make me take a deep long look at my life. Even years later I clearly recall that experience and how unnerved I was by this man's probing questions. Yet without that push in the right direction, where would I be today? Would I still be hiding behind the horses and running from relationships? If I had not changed I would have never stepped out and met this wonderful man who is my husband today. How awesome God is to step in even when we try to argue with His methods.

Does everyone try to find something to hide behind? Probably. Are we living life to the fullest? Not if we are hiding behind walls of self-protection we aren't. These are questions I still have to ask myself from time to time making me take a long hard look as to whether I am walking the road God has laid before me or gotten off the narrow path. God still places markers, people, and angels to remind me of the way. There have been so many times I could not possibly count them. I am sure there are even more that happen daily that I am not even aware of.

I am also sure He sends them for you. We just have to learn to look at these "divine appointments" and ask ourselves, "Why has my path crossed this person's path?" I think you would be amazed if you took a bit of time out of the day to take a deep breath and discover what amazing angels we walk among and how many incredible people the Lord has placed around us.

Do I hide behind the horses anymore? No, my last one died a year ago and my heart breaks sometimes as I miss them. But I am blessed to be around them if I wish. My son has blessed my life by keeping some horses around. It still makes me feel like a new person when I am allowed to have at least part of a day to enjoy the horse's company. That unconditional love they send has a way of opening our hearts if we will allow it to, but they are not meant to keep us from facing the issues in our lives.

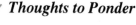

Thoughts to Ponder

Are you hiding behind something such as work, children, drugs or alcohol? The list can go on; it doesn't have to be an animal. Maybe yours is something else or maybe you have put something in place instead of the Lord. What drives you to get up every morning and face the world?

I challenge you to take a deep look into your life. Give God the opportunity to speak to you. He is listening; all you have to do is talk to Him. He is nearer than you think. Enjoy the peace He has for you when you draw near to Him. Nothing compares to the relationship you can have with your loving Heavenly Father!

Thank You, Heavenly Father for sending me Your comforting representatives in my time of need. Help me to receive them as a gift from You.

Chapter 4

ANGELS TAKE TIME

I t seems when we pray many times we think that instantly
the prayer is answered at that second. Our prayers give the
angels the opportunity to work on our behalf, but sometimes
we have to give them time and wait on the Lord.

At times we need to be reminded that Jesus spoke:

*Verily I say unto you, whatsoever ye shall bind on
earth shall be bound in heaven; and whatsoever ye
shall loose on earth shall be loosed in heaven. Again I
say unto you, that if two of you shall agree on earth as
touching anything that they shall ask, it shall be done
for them of my Father which is in heaven.* (Matthew
18:18-19 KJV)

We can see from this scripture we bind things here and
then it is sent to heaven as our prayers for God to disperse
His angels to do His bidding. Our prayers don't stay down
here on earth and just happen to resolve themselves. That is
not what the Word of God says. Jesus lets us know that they
rise to His heavenly Father who is in heaven. That is where
the prayers are answered.

Daniel prayed to God and it took twenty-one days for the angel to answer his prayer. The angel came and talked to Daniel about why it took him so long to bring a result.

In those days I Daniel was mourning three full weeks….Then said he said unto me, fear not, Daniel: for from the first day that thou didst set thine heart to understand and to chasten thyself before thy God, thy works were heard, and I am come for thy words. But the prince of the kingdom of Persia withstood me one and twenty days but, lo, Michael, one of the chief princes came to help me; and I remained there with the kings of Persian. (Daniel 10:2, 12-13)

This is the story where Daniel needed God to intercede. When we pray this it shows us that our prayers go to heaven to where God's angels are able to start working on the request. They do, however, have opposition from Satan and the fallen angels. So the angels working on our prayers have to fight their way back to answer our prayers.

We are living on a fallen earth and even though we have been redeemed from the curse by the Lord Jesus Christ, that does not mean we are exempt from the fight on behalf of our prayer sent to God. How many times do you say a prayer and you know all the scriptures about having faith and yet you do not see immediate results? This story God has given us about Daniel helps us understand the reason for some of those delays.

When our nephews came to live with us, I suggested that they start keeping a journal of their requests from God and record how and when their prayers are answered. The boys were excited to see how quickly God responded when they logged the time. I challenge you to ledger your prayers and keep track of the time it takes for God to answer your prayers. You may also be pleasantly surprised.

A couple years ago I ended up in the hospital with an allergic reaction which took away my eye sight. This was not the first time in my life I'd lost my sight. When I was sixteen, I mixed bleach and dish soap to clean the baby's bottles and the bottle exploded in my face and I was blinded. I spent a lengthy time with no eyesight. Now, years later, I found myself unable to read or even see my key to place it in the door.

I prayed and made a petition to God and had it stapled to my wall of healing scriptures. This blindness left me without work for almost four months. I am a cosmetologist and no one wants a blind hairstylist working on their hair. Can't say as I blame them!

One day I went to my music room, closed the door, and stood in the dark because though I could not really "see" the light hurt my eyes. I had a long talk with the Lord. I reminded Him that many years ago He had given me my sight back when I had prayed. It did not come over night at that time, but He was honorable and answered my prayers in about a year. I reminded God of His healing that many years ago, and I told Him I believed He would give me that healing again. I could sing and play my guitar without my eye sight, but I knew Jesus healed all that came to Him and I was going to stand on that. My prayer was sent to heaven and I waited for my healing.

While I was waiting, I wrote on a paper in large red marker, "There's a Treasurer in Every Trial," and stapled it to the wall in front of my computer. Thank goodness for computers because you can make all the letters larger so you can read them even with impaired vision. When my husband read what I posted, he expressed to me that he hoped it was true. I reassured him God is always faithful. We now had to wait, though I agreed it wasn't easy to do so patiently.

I was sent from one eye specialist to another and was told I would know I was going to get my eyesight back when I could see the leaves on the trees. Later, when I did receive my sight, the top specialist told me how surprised he was that I actually did. He said no one he knew of had received their sight back after they'd had as much damage as I had from the blistering in my eyes. He was amazed! God shows His love, grace and mercy again!

However, as I waited expectantly, the time seemed to drag on. I decided to go and visit my daughter, as the doctor suggested, so I would stop worrying about my clients, which I couldn't do anything about. My daughter is a nurse and had the doctor's phone number if something else went wrong. I seemed to keep having allergic reactions to everything they tried to give me. So off I went to stay with Lisa for a week or so.

Each day I just hung around, rested and played with the dog. It was great to get out of state so I wouldn't feel guilty about not being at work. Funny how we seem to think we are "atlas women," isn't it? Well, I'm here to tell you we are not! We have to wait on the Lord and His angels as they fight to fulfill our prayers. One morning as I sat out on the front porch enjoying a cup of coffee with my girlfriend, I could see the leaves on the tree closest to me. They weren't just a green blob of a tree, like a painted picture; I could see the detail in them.

"I can see the leaves!" I told her.

She smiled and said, "Oh, yes."

Again I said, "No, you don't understand, I can actually see the individual leaves on this tree. The doctors told me I would know that I would receive my eyesight back when I could see the leaves on the trees!"

What an exciting day that was, yet by the afternoon I couldn't see the leaves anymore. I knew God had given me a glimpse of His mercy, and I thanked Him all day, knowing my healing was on the way. My angels must have been fighting overtime to bring it to me. In Jude it discusses of how Michael the archangel was dealing with the devil.

Yet Michael the archangel, when contending with the devil he disputed about the body of Moses, "durst not bring against him a railing accusation," but said, "The Lord rebuke thee." (Jude 1:9)

When we speak prayers, it sends the angels into action! God's angels can and will defeat the devil on our behalf!

Have you given the angels anything to do lately? Are your angels bored because you don't ask them to do anything on your behalf?

Remember, while we wait on the Lord that He accomplishes our petitions and prayers, He has the best in mind for us. He is our Heavenly Father and the angels are His to command. If we are the King's Kids, we can patiently wait, reassured He is working on our behalf. Praise Him while you wait for your answers, don't complain, speak the end result and keep your eyes waiting expectantly! The angels are fighting your battles, and sometimes it takes time.

Walk by faith, not by sight. (2 Corinthians 5:7)

We just need to get out of the way and let God work. After all, we can't do anything anyway. He's the One who is in control.

Thoughts to Ponder

When we speak prayers God sends the angels into action!
Have you given the angels anything to do lately?
Are your angels bored because you don't ask for them to do anything on your behalf?

33

Have you ever said a prayer, known all the scriptures about having faith, and yet you do not see immediate results? I challenge you to ledger your prayers, praise Him while you wait for your answers, don't complain, speak the end result, and keep your eyes waiting expectantly! Keep track of the time it takes for God to answer your prayers. You may be surprised!

Pray: *Thank You, Father that You send Your angels to do Your will as You answer my prayers. Help me to truly walk by faith, not by sight as I wait expectantly for Your answers.*

Chapter 5

GUIDE ME HOLY SPIRIT

When I was very young before my mother became ill, she would read from the Bible every night. It was a time I really did enjoy. We would all sit around like a hen with her little chicks expecting to get something exciting from this book that was full of the promises from God. This was the beginning of my search for God's hand in my life and the Holy Spirit to guide me through my journey in this life.

Time went by and many trials came in our lives even as children, which I share in great detail in my book, "On Fire for God." Those early years of listening to the stories of the Bible left me constantly wondering what else was out there besides what I saw happening around me. My heart was always searching for that something else which no one seemed to be able to share with me. When I asked I was told to read the Bible because the answers to all my questions were there. I can see now that what they said was indeed true. The Holy Spirit has led me to search for the truth by searching through the Scriptures. The only way I could satisfy that driving force in my life of, "there has to be more," was to seek the truth. Do you understand that kind of constant drive to know God more?

I was always one of those children that wanted to know why. I truly wanted to know. I couldn't understand why someone couldn't just explain it to me. The "whys" filled my days and nights as I saw the wonders God placed in my sight. The sun and moon, the stars and the clouds, the list went on as I could see the color He painted in the flowers and the trees. There had to be more to life when there were so many wonderful things all around me. Why was I so desperately longing to know what else God had for me?

When I was five I understood that Jesus had died for my sins and accepted Him as my Savor and this drove my passion for knowing Him to an ultimate height of questions, what else? I suppose when I think back to all the things God has led me through, He has given me the answers to those questions one adventure at a time.

Being burned to the point of death when I was eight years old and going to heaven to be in the Lord's presence was one of those experiences that helped fulfill the yearning in my soul to know Him more intimately. When I was grown I came into His presence again. He told me this was the reason I was born and gave me directions to be a faith builder. That was another time He fulfilled that need to be close with my Lord. I have to tell you there is nothing like it. I long for the time I once again am in His presence where there is no pain and we have no needs. His light and love shining through us is the ultimate fulfillment of life. My times in heaven are more truth to me than the life I lead here. I long to fulfill the mission He has sent me to accomplish and look forward to joining Him again in heaven when my work here is done.

I will not leave you comfortless: I will come to you. Yet in a little while, and the world seeth me no more; but ye see me: because I live, ye shall live also. At that day ye shall know that I am in my Father, and ye in me, and I in you. (John 14:18-20)

Jesus explains that He will not leave us without the comfort of His company and guidance. He will send us the **Comforter** who is the **Holy Ghost**. Can you imagine how wonderful that is to know the same **Comforter** that lived in Jesus? Because Jesus was willing to give His life for us, He said the Father would send that **Comforter** to reside in each and every one of us who are willing to accept Jesus Christ as our Lord. Why would we ever turn down such an amazing gift?

*But that **Comforter**, which is the **Holy Ghost**, whom the Father will send in my name, He shall teach you all things, and bring all things to your remembrance, whatsoever I have said unto you. Peace I leave with you, my peace I give unto you not as the world giveth, give I unto you. Let not your heart be troubled, neither let it be afraid.* (John 14:26-27 emphasis added)

Years ago when my children were about grown, I felt led to attend this full gospel church that believed in all the gifts the Lord has given. Now we know God is eternal and He never changes. The Bible still applies today the same as it did the day God inspired it to be written. Yet at times we find some of the gifts are said to be for just that time, not now. I do not believe that any way, shape or form. I believe what God has put into place for us in the Bible is still available for us today. I think Satan is trying to keep us from getting the blessing God has for us by getting us to believe the lie. I don't believe that and I hope you don't either. Why would we take certain parts out of the Bible and keep others? Wouldn't that be compromising God's Word and promises? Once it starts, when and how do we stop it? That's a tough one isn't it, especially when we are searching for the truth?

When I came into this full gospel church there was energy unlike any other I had experienced in the other churches I attended. I didn't want to miss what was going on, but I didn't want to be in the front either so I sat about half way back in the church. You could sense the presence of the Lord in this place. It was late in the service when a couple came into the church. One notices when it is that late. They also looked as if they came from a different area in the world, not dressed like we are in this country. Suddenly a woman stood up and started speaking in tongues. I had never heard anyone speaking in tongues before and felt a bit like a fish out of the water as they say. Everyone was very still. No one interpreted the word spoken. The woman who had spoken it said she knew it was what God wanted her to speak, and it was for someone in the room. The pastor explained that those were words that were the angels' language were to be spoken with an interpretation when in public (1 Corinthians 14:28). He explained that it was unusual that there was no immediate interpretation, but he would proceed with his sermon allowing God to do what He wanted concerning that message.

When the service came to an end, the couple who had come in late quickly went to the woman who had spoken in tongues and started speaking to her in their native language. The woman explained she could not understand what they were saying, but they insisted she had spoken to them earlier when she stood up. They explained they felt led by the Holy Spirit to stop as they were passing by the church and came in just in time for her to stand up and speak the words that gave the answer they had prayed for.

I had been led by the Holy Spirit to come to this church that very same day and so had this couple who needed an answer from God. If the Holy Spirit, who glorifies Jesus, had not guided me that day and I had not listened, I would have missed this wonderful experience of God's hand working for many through speaking in the angels' language (1 Corinthians 13:1). God is so good to answer our questions when we truly are in prayer and search for His face. He wants us to include Him in everything we experience in life.

What gave me the comfort over those years when I was struggling through trying to find the truth? I know it was the Holy Spirit which Jesus sent to comfort me. He will comfort you also when you receive the Lord as your Savior. Ask for His guidance and He will step up and lead you the way you need to go. He will answer the questions you have when you need an answer.

The Holy Spirit is there any time you need guidance, just ask and allow Him to help you with your walk. Listen to that still small voice throughout your day and be blessed by the pearls He places in your life daily.

Thoughts to Ponder

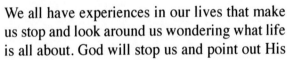

We all have experiences in our lives that make us stop and look around us wondering what life is all about. God will stop us and point out His wonderful world to us if we will heed His still small voice. He wants to answer each and every one of our questions, too. God our Heavenly Father wants so much to be in communication with you and me that He sent first His Son and then His Holy Spirit to communicate His thoughts and love to us.

Ask for His guidance and He will step up and lead you the way you need to go. He will answer the questions you have when you need an answer. The Holy Spirit is there any time you need guidance. You just need to ask and then allow Him to help you with your walk. Listen to that small still voice throughout your day and be blessed by the pearls He places in your life daily.

Pray: *Lord, I pray open my ears that I might hear Your still small voice as I search for Your truth. Thank You for the peace and comfort You give as I come into Your presence and wait for You to commune with me. Thank*

You for Your Holy Spirit. I ask Him to guide me today as I go through my daily activities.

Chapter 6

BLESSED FRIENDS

Through my life I have been blessed by so many people and I wish to share a couple of these delightful godly women that I am proud to call my friends. We wonder how we are so blessed to have these friends in our life that last a lifetime. I would say to you, the Holy Ghost and God's angels have sent them your way so enjoy and appreciate them. Let me give you a couple of examples of how blessed I have been.

At one point in my life I was hunting for a place to put a new salon and nothing seemed to be available at the time in our town. It was just before the building boom hit and the spaces were very sparse. I prayed about it and God led us to this building which seemed to meet our needs. My husband, being the saint he is, worked hard at getting the salon together in a timely manner.

Once I was in the building I could see I needed someone who was able to do everything I don't do. All I do is hair, I do not do pedicures, facials, nails, and etc.; hair is my thing. My shop was not big enough to add these features so once again I started praying for God to send someone who did everything I did not do. I knew it was a big order to ask for a salon like that next to me, but with God nothing is impossible.

At the same time Flo, a delightful Philippine lady, was praying for the same thing. She needed a place to be able to open her salon which did everything I did not do. Flo could do hair but it was not her thing. My husband was excited after he met Flo and her husband and quickly informed me of what a nice family they were. I was blessed to have her salon next to mine.

Within the week of Flo opening her shop next to mine, I came home from out of town with food poisoning. Boy! No one would wish that on their worst enemy! It was terrible and yet I had to work. Flo was a God-send in my path as they say. She was over every hour trying to see what she could do to help me. She brought me chicken noodle soup and all sorts of teas trying to make me feel better. She has a servant's heart which is the best kind. The Holy Ghost certainly led her to my path. I have been blessed to call Flo an awesome friend that has become like my sister.

Ecclesiastes 3:1 says, "To everything there is a season, and a time to every purpose under the heaven." This reminds us the Lord has seasons for our life. He sends the people we need as friends to meet the needs of each season. I am proud to share this part of my life with you and pray it encourages you to enjoy the friends you have while you have them.

Kay was another that I was blessed to call my friend before she went home to be with the Lord. The Holy Spirit would bring to mind Kay when she was in need of something and I was blessed by God to have this special connection. On my lunch hour one day, I felt I should go to the store for Kay. I had just found out she had cancer and wasn't sure what was good for her, but off to the store I went and asked the Lord to guide me. What was God sending me to get for her?

I started where the veggie and fruit section was and picked up a few things, but felt led to keep traveling through the store. I came by a pizza display and felt the nudge of the Holy Spirit to pick up a couple pizzas. I quietly told the Holy Spirit, I was sure pizza wasn't on her list of good foods. As I walked on I felt that prodding even stronger and returned to pick up a couple pizzas as I said to myself, *Okay, I asked for help and I have to listen to what God tells me, not what I think.* Out the door I went with all the treasures which God had led me to purchase for my friend, including the pizzas.

When I dropped by Kay's I could see she was exhausted. I unloaded all the groceries and she said how nice it was I brought groceries for her on a day she didn't feel like shopping. Then when she saw the pizzas, she sat down and started crying.

"How did you know?" she asked me.

I felt lost and explained I didn't understand. I told her I had no idea why God told me to bring those pizzas but He'd insisted. She told me it was her youngest son's birthday and she had promised him pizza on his birthday, but she was not well enough to go to the store. Wow! Did I feel silly for trying to second guess the Lord as His Holy Spirit was guiding me. I was trying to run by my own senses, not by His prodding.

Time went by and there were many nights the Lord would wake me and tell me Kay needed to have prayer on her behalf. Up I would jump and find healing and comforting scriptures as the Lord led me. The next day we would discuss what kind of evening she'd had and I would let her know at what time I was awake praying for her. I found it a privilege to pray for her in the wee hours of the night. I don't suggest you ask for a gift like this one where the Lord keeps you connected to a person who is ill unless you truly are willing to walk the walk. I can tell you it is not an easy one to undertake. Your life will be changed by this constant awareness of the suffering person's needs.

When the time came for Hospice to be involved, Kay's husband explained that I would probably be in and out at all hours of the night and day with Kay. By that time he had figured out the Lord had a given us this special bond and that

I was willing to go the extra mile with Kay. I was grateful of this grace he offered me that allowed me to come and spend the time needed to intercede on her behalf. The first night we had her settled in before nine in the Hospice center. They were so wonderful. I went home to get some rest assured they would call if I was needed.

It was almost eleven that night when I heard Kay's voice in my spirit. I heard her voice as if she was there in the same room with me. Out of bed I jumped. I had not heard her voice before this time. It had been the Lord that had woke me up in the past asking for me to pray for her, but this time it was Kay directly. I quickly threw on my clothes and prepared to leave. When my husband asked what was going on, I told him I'd heard Kay calling and I had to go back to Hospice. I told him I didn't know when I would return, but I would call him later and let him know what was going on.

I was buzzed into Hospice and they told me Kay was restless. I told them I thought I'd spend some time with her. When I came into the room I told Kay I heard her calling and reassured her everything was fine. I discussed all the things we had put in place, preparing for this situation. I asked her if she would like me to read some of the books we had brought in and she shook her head yes. I read until I fell asleep sometime early the next morning. Her husband woke me when he came in the next morning. Kay had finally fallen asleep.

Earlier in the year my daughter came to live in Arizona. I wondered why God had sent her to our part of the country. She was living in Illinois and we were in Arizona, but I did enjoy getting to know my daughter as an adult and am very proud to call her my daughter. She is a compassionate woman of God and when Kay got very ill and ended up in Hospice; my daughter did a great job of keeping my business going. I knew then why God had sent Lisa to be with us. She was such a blessing at a time of crisis in my life.

Time flies by us all and I can't believe how quickly it comes and goes, but I challenge you to take a look at the people God has placed in your life. I could go on and on about all the wonderful women I have been privileged to have in my life, and I am sure you have also. But if you are a person who does not have any friends, I will give you a little insight. It takes a friend to be a friend and it takes time invested in each other's lives to make a cherished friend that lasts a lifetime. All we have to do is ask the Lord to guide us and He will pick the friends for us.

Be aware of how the Holy Ghost is leading you and acknowledge you are worthy of these new friends. God does not make junk and you are His creation. He knows what you need. I know we all think we are busy, but when all is said and done, all we really have are the memories of our family and friends. Make them count, allow God to lead you by His Holy Spirit, and you will not make a wrong turn. He will keep you on the right path if you are willing to listen and follow His lead.

Thoughts to Ponder

We all have special people God brings into our lives. Take a few moments and list those precious friends God has gifted you with. Thank Him for each one of them. Then take the time to send a note thanking them as well. If your special friends have already gone to be with the Lord, bless their families by telling them what a wonderful gift their loved one was to you.

Ask the Holy Spirit to bring to mind any of your friends that may need a special word or gift from you each and every day. You will be amazed at how easy it is to give of yourself when you see what even the smallest gesture of caring can do.

Pray: *Father God, thank You for Your Holy Spirit. I ask Him to guide me today and every day so that I can be a blessing to those special people You have brought into my life. Use me Lord, to bless them in a special way.*

Chapter 7

GOD RINGS

O n this particular day I was busy, and yet I can't say
I was accomplishing anything in particular. My ears
started to ring. I think we can all agree it is very annoying
when that happens. You can't think of other things when
you hear that shrill screeching noise in your ears. I opened
my mouth like you do on the planes when you are changing
altitudes and your ears can't handle the pressure, but this
didn't help. I move my head around as if I thought doing
exercises would help, but to no avail.

Finally I said, "Lord, what is going on?"

The moment I asked that question the ringing stopped! I
quit the silly gestures I thought might help stop the unceasing
ringing in my ears.

"What a strange thing," I thought to myself.

I continued on like nothing had happened. I hate to admit
that I can't remember what was so important that day to
make me so busy that I couldn't understand what the Lord
was telling me.

Why do we run through life and forget to smell the roses
as they say? We busy ourselves and run in circles, starting
one project and then another wondering why we are worn
out at the end of the day. Our eyes are full of distractions

and if we are not careful to stay on task, they will run our lives instead.

For some reason I seemed to be oblivious as to why the change in my ears occurred and I dismissed it. It had not been but a couple minutes and the ringing came back. I'm sure that the terrible screeching was even louder the second time.

I stopped and said out loud, "Lord, what in the world is this about?"

Immediately the ringing stopped. Now He had my attention and I stopped doing whatever silly thing it was that was so important it took my attention away from what the Lord was trying to tell me. I thought about the passage of the Bible I had read that morning.

And he said, Go Forth, and stand upon the mount before the Lord. And, behold, the Lord passed by, and a great and strong wind rent the mountains, and brake in pieces the rocks before the Lord; but the Lord was not in the wind; and after the wind an earthquake: but the Lord was not in the earthquake: And after the earthquake a fire: but the Lord was not in the fire: and after the fire a still small voice. (1 Kings 19:11-12)

My thoughts flashed back to a time when I was about twelve and I had heard a voice call my name. It was when I was mowing the lawn. I heard it as clearly as if the person was standing next to me. The mower was very loud, but the voice over-rode the sound of the mower. I looked around and couldn't see anyone and the voice called my name again.

In my first book, "On Fire for God," I explain how I was burned and couldn't tell where sound was coming from. I turned off the mower and went into the house to see if someone was calling me. Everyone told me no, and sent me back to finish the mowing since it was my turn to mow. They acted like I was a bit strange and I just dismissed them thinking the same about them. I knew I heard the voice calling me. Back to the mower I went and started my task for the day again. The voice came back calling my name again. Once again I turned off the mower and went to ask everyone the same question. They acted like I was trying to get out of my job, but I wasn't. I actually enjoyed mowing the lawn.

The mowing still needed to be finished so one more time I started the mower. Just as I was finishing my task, I heard the voice again. I laughed thinking, "It must be you, Lord; no one else is calling me." The voice did not return and I've often wondered what it was that He was trying to tell me. I was only thinking of how I could hear His voice over the mower as if it wasn't running and not what He wanted to tell me.

As I came back to the present and the ringing in my ears I was experiencing again, it reminded me of how God can talk to us anytime if we are not too busy to listen. I asked the Lord if He was talking to me. I received no sign immediately but when I started to walk away, the ringing started again.

I spoke out loud and said, "Lord, I know You are trying to communicate to me. I apologize I did not listen and receive what You were trying to tell me when I was mowing the lawn so many years ago."

As I waited for His response, I wondered how my life might have changed if I had listened to His voice that day. I felt humbled because I was not listening with my spiritual ears to what He had to say to me. It is sad the Lord had to ring me like a telephone to get me to stop and pay attention. My life has been changed by this experience with God and the Holy Spirit to guide me.

Now when my ears begin to ring, I immediately begin to pray. When I don't know what to pray, I ask the Holy Spirit to guide my prayers. When I have prayed for the situation God wants for me to pray for, my ears stop ringing. Sometimes He brings people to mind and other times I continue to pray until the ringing stops. People come to me and tell me of how the Lord saved them from a disaster that happened the same time I was praying for them. The Lord placed the ringing in my ears to get me to stop and pray and intercede for others.

My daughter called me several years ago and asked why I thought her ears were ringing. She told me it had been ringing on and off for days and she couldn't stand it. Being the person I was at the time, I didn't feel I could share what might seem a bit crazy, so I hesitated to tell her of why my ears ring. She heard the hesitation in my voice even though I was on the phone, and insisted I tell her what I was thinking. I shared with her my experience and said it may sound crazy, but it was the truth. I told her it might not work for her, but I felt I was supposed to share this revelation.

She took what I told her and said she would try it out. I prayed that the Lord would give her confirmation on this kind of prayer life. Within a couple days she called back and confirmed that she had prayed when the ringing came in her ears. When people she knew came to mind, she prayed for them. Later she found that at the very same time those people she had prayed for were in situations where only God's intervention could have saved them.

There are many different ways that God talks to us when we learn to listen. Some women have shared that when they are having an itching on their arm, they feel they are to pray and intercede for someone. Others say their hands itch or their noses itch. There are many ways that others have found God works to reach them. I challenge you to be aware of how God might get your attention to spend time with you. There are several different medical reasons peoples ears ring and all sorts of reasons the doctors will tell you. However, I want to challenge you to take time with the Lord, get in His Word, and pray.

Speaking the Word of God out of the Bible enables the angels to do God's work. This intervention may show others how only by God's hand have they been blessed through a terrible situation. Listen when you hear that small still voice. Take time to hear what wonderful things God has for you when you draw near to Him. Allow the Holy Spirit to guide you and His angels to work on your behalf.

What is it then? I will pray with the spirit: and I will pray with the understanding also; I will sing with the spirit, and I will sing with the understanding also. (1 Corinthians 14:15)

Thoughts to Ponder

How does God get your attention when you need to pray for something or someone?

Are you quiet and still so you can hear when God does talk to you or do you miss the small still voice of the Holy Spirit talking to you?

Are your ears ringing to the sound of the Lord?

Is God reminding you not to be so busy and to take time for those who need prayer?

I challenge you to hear when God calls, don't miss out on God's blessing.

Pray today: *God, please give me ears to hear Your still small voice and give me wisdom to pray for those You need me to intercede for.*

Chapter 8

COMPLACENCY

W e had our first album, "I'm Gonna' Sing," and I was
feeling pretty good about our accomplishment. I
could hear that still small voice within me saying, "Don't be
complacent!" I have learned since then to not feel too good
about my accomplishments. They are because of the grace of
God and not because of me.

Every Wednesday I would travel over to Litchfield Park,
about an hour and half from my home, and we would work on
our music. My sister had her business office out of her home so
it was easier for me to travel to her than the other way around.

This particular day I was headed up I-10 trying to convince God that I was not complacent and that I was making
a difference in this world. I know this seems craziness, but
let's face it, we all argue with the Holy Spirit, that voice inside
us, when we want to continue doing what we want. So many
times we try to convince God to agree with us instead of the
other way around. I knew I would be affected because of my
actions or reactions to His still small voice, and still at times I
seemed to go on with what I wanted to do instead of heeding
His quiet gentle voice.

That voice within me clearly said to turn off and travel
up one of the side roads. Well anyone that has ever ridden

with me knows I don't like to get lost. I'm talking to the Holy Spirit by now and informing Him that I didn't think that road went across the reservation and I could possibly end up on the wrong road getting lost. I know it is ridiculous to argue with Him, but I still find myself doing it at times. When will I learn that He is trying to keep me safe or teach me something that I need to get my mind and heart around? Thank goodness God is not through with me and He hasn't given up on me. I'm a work in progress and there is still hope for me.

As I turned off in obedience to His voice, the anxiety rose up within me. I slowly traveled down the road all the while hoping He would tell me He only wanted to see if I would be obedient. Of course He does want our obedience, but that was not His full plan in this case. Thoughts ran through my mind telling me to turn around, go back to where I was on familiar ground, and go on to my sister's house as planned.

"What if you're late?" my mind started to ask.

That should always be a clue that it's not from God—if you hear "What If?" or, "But!"

I traveled a few miles realizing that God was truly making a point. I had to ride this trip out until He gave me further directions because I am now in totally unfamiliar territory out in the middle of nowhere with no idea where I would end up. I approached a small Indian village and slowly drive through.

Suddenly, I hear, "Pull over, look around, and tell Me what do you see?"

I quickly noticed the grave yard which I wanted to pretend I didn't notice, and then scanned over to where the children were playing in the school yard. I told God I saw the school and the children playing. I knew God was working on me about being complacent and that the children playing were not going to be the point of contact that He wanted me to think on.

I felt the silence all around me until my eyes once again focused on the small sad grave yard. Echoes of sadness rolled over me as I thought of all the lost ones in that grave yard.

The Indians do not always bury their loved ones like we do. This day someone had placed their loved one up on stilts and they were holding a burial ceremony.

"Such sad faces," I thought as I stared at them, heavy in my heart.

I heard clearly, "If you do not stop being complacent I will take you out of this place. You are as the dead when you are not doing My will and not being obedient! Do your work, the harvest is ripe, and you are here for this season! Do not think it is because of your works, but because of Mine. The glory belongs to Me, God Almighty!"

My heart felt as if it were broken. I had been complacent and had not kept God's will first in my life. I sat and wept asking for His forgiveness. When I could see through my tears, I traveled on down the road God had placed before me to travel that day. Eventually I recognized where the road intersected to one I could cross the valley on.

When I arrived at my sister's, I told her of the morning I'd had with God as I traveled over to see her. We both cried and prayed to God, humbly asking for Him to be our Manager for The Faith Sisters singing group. We asked God to guide our every move and not allow us to ever get in the way or become complacent again.

I am reminded also that as long as I allow God to drive me through this wonderful life He has placed here for my enjoyment, I will be safe and sound. But if I get behind the wheel and try to drive myself, I will always crash and it will not take long to happen. God will get my attention one way or the other. If I am in struggle mode and not staying in His peace, He will not intervene and will allow me to stay in the situation until I stop struggling. As any good parent does, He will wait until I am ready for His help, then and only then will He step in.

Our Father knows what's best for us and it will not benefit any of us to argue with Him. He loves us. If the sparrows don't worry about what they are to eat every day, then how much more will God feed and clothe us (see Matthew 6:26). I don't see any birds wringing their wings saying, "Oh my, I can't find any worms to eat today."

When I think of that moment when the Lord had to take me to the grave yard to get my attention, it still touches my heart and soul. I can honestly tell you God has made it clear that we can be busy doing things that we think are important, but they may not really be what God expects from us. I understand that God searches our hearts and wants us to do His will because of how much we love Him. However, if we get busy thinking we are doing good things for Him, but we haven't sought if that is what the Holy Spirit is trying to nudge us to do to, it may not really be making a difference for the Lord.

Don't allow life to make you complacent. It will move you away from God's will, and when we move away from God's will we get into the snares of the wicked one. Keep your eyes on the Lord and allow Him to lead you where He gives many blessings and His mercy abounds much.

Thoughts to Ponder

Look up the word complacent and write out the definition. Does complacent describe where you are right now in relationship to what God wants you to do for Him?

Pray and ask God to show you any areas of your life where you may have become complacent and therefore ineffective for Him.

Complacency = a feeling of smug or
un critical satisfaction w/ oneself or
one's achievements, self satisfaction,
self gratification; self-regard

55

Chapter 9

I'M GRATEFUL

One day you wake up and realize your life is more than half over and wonder if it has meaning. Have I made a difference in others' lives? I am grateful for life's trials that have allowed me the opportunity to grow spiritually and comfort others. Each day should be as they say, "an attitude of gratitude," and an opportunity to "pay-it-forward."

Pay-it-forward means we show acts of kindness to those around us. A very special friend of mine told me, it is like the Lord has given us one great big living room and sometimes we have to stand up and let someone else sit down. That has stuck in my head. I can see what that would be like if everyone would think that way. Let's face it, wouldn't it be like heaven?

Remember when chivalry was still in the foremost of men's minds, when women enjoyed being a woman, as I do? The men were happy to stand and let a woman sit down, and a man would hurry to open the door for a woman. I still see that chivalry and my life is so blessed by it. I look forward to telling the man it is so nice to see a gentleman.

My sister once asked me, "Why do the men rush to open the doors for you and they don't for me?"

"I think it is in the way you view yourself," I told her.

She always rushed and didn't give the gentlemen a chance to open the door. Many times we women act like we neither need nor want any assistance from a man. Women's lib has made men fearful that if he does open the door he may be reprimanded instead of thanked by some out-of-sorts ungrateful female. How sad is that!

If you remember you are a child of God you will "place that impression out to the universe" as they say. One can tell how a person feels about themselves when they enter a room. We have seen people either light up the party or bring it down simply by their presence. Incredible isn't it? They walk in and are allowed to affect another person's emotions. Yet we are supposed to be the commander of our own emotions. Especially as children of God, we should be the ones setting the atmosphere of any room we walk into.

Do you know you are a child of God? If we are a child of God's then we are princes and princesses and we are to be held in high esteem, even by ourselves. It is important for us to see ourselves in the light that God has provided us through Jesus Christ who died on the cross for us. Christ paid the price so we should view this as the gift given us by God, our loving Heavenly Father. When we understand how much God loves us, we will hold ourselves to a higher standard and that light that is within us goes out to all those within our area of influence. We show how we feel about ourselves by our walk, the sparkle in our eyes, and by the love that emulates from our very presence in the room.

My sister and I had come from a home that had suppressed love so my sister had a tough time accepting how much God loved her. The words spoken to her from our mother when she was young had imprinted on her soul and what a scar it had made. Our words either bring life or bring hurt and pain to others.

I told my sister when we were on our last singing tour I was going to start calling her Queeny until she got the gist that she was the King's Kid. It did help and she started giggling whenever she started trying to do something she was not supposed to do like gather the trash in the hotel room, make the beds, and the list would go on. I would say, "Now Queeny, is that something the King's Kid should be struggling with?" It was great to see her blossom as she began to realize that she was loved and was the King's Kid. Somehow she was able to get the grasp of it when I called her Queeny.

I have seen it work for others who don't feel like they deserve to be the King's child. Do any of us really deserve it? Certainly not, but through nothing short of grace we have been adopted into the family of God. What a great God we serve don't you think? Consider all the wonderful benefits He so freely gives us.

The LORD bless thee, and keep thee: the LORD make his face shine upon thee, and be gracious unto thee: the LORD lift up his countenance upon thee, and give thee peace. (Numbers 6:24-26)

When we see God loves us so much that He told Moses to have Aaron speak that blessing in Numbers 6:24-26 over the children of Israel, we can see God has wonderful things planned for His children. We can also begin to understand why God asks us to be kind to one another as it says in Colossians 3:12-13.

Put on therefore, as the elect of God, holy and beloved, bowels of mercies, kindness, humbleness of mind, meekness, longsuffering; Forbearing one another, and forgiving one another...even as Christ forgave you.

Sun shines on our lives when we look passed ourselves and start helping others. One cannot stay depressed when we step out of the box and have the heart to ask, "What can I do to help you?" If we seriously do this without expecting anything in return, we cannot stay depressed. I challenge anyone to be depressed when you make a child smile as you give them a gift from your heart. It is almost impossible. The love of the God will rise up within you, remind you of delightful times, and you will want to pass your joy on to others.

I am surrounded everyday by people that love the Lord and are willing to make a difference in someone else's life. I am sure you are also. We are able to find wonderful people if we are looking for the light in others. We need to be prepared to make a difference in someone else's life each and every day. It is the little things in life that make the most difference and they certainly do add up to big things.

Step out in faith knowing the Lord will guide you to make a difference. I am very grateful to be able to pay-it-forward. I feel we all have much to be grateful for, living in the land of the free, and the home of the brave—America. Determine to reflect your grateful heart every day by paying-it-forward and blessing others as you have been blessed.

Thoughts to Ponder

Do you know you are a child of God?
If you are a child of God then realize you are the King's Kid. You are a prince or a princess.
Do you hold yourself in high esteem as a child of God?

It is important to see yourself in the light of the gift God provided through Jesus Christ who died on the cross for you.

Have you received that gift of God's love?

When you understand how much God loves you, you will not only hold yourself to a higher standard, you will also want to take that gift God offers, and pay-it-forward to those all around you.

Read John 3:16 and Romans 10:9-11. If you have never accepted God's gift of love, pray today and ask Jesus to be your Lord and Savior.

Pray: *Father God, I believe that You sent Your Son Jesus to die for me for the forgiveness of my sins. Please forgive me for my sins. I want to receive Your free gift of salvation and eternal life. I want to be Your child as Your word says I can. Thank You Father for Your gift of love.*

Chapter 10

HOSPITAL APARTMENT

R ecently I was traveling through O'Hare Airport in Chicago and had a layover. Whenever I have what appears to be an interruption in my plans as I travel, I look at it as an opportunity for God to show me something. Sometimes it is as simple as talking to someone who needs a kind word. This day, as I sat and watched the crowd with my coffee and a muffin in hand, a young lady with two children in tow was trying to find her way through the bustling airport. It brought me back to a time when I was struggling with two small children by myself.

I was married and had my son, James by the time I was sixteen, had my daughter Lisa at seventeen, and was divorced at eighteen. My husband had post war syndrome and other drug issues from severe trauma from an auto accident and the children and I were not in a safe place with him. A sad but true situation; more said about this subject in my book, "On Fire for God." I had worked since I was fifteen at restaurants, but had no formal training under my belt. My son was two and my daughter about six months, when I was divorced and facing life alone to raise two small children. I can remember asking God how in the world I was going to take care of myself and my two children.

His response to me was, "I take care of widows and children and you have been a widow for some time and I will care for you."

I can still hear His voice as clearly as I did that day when He spoke that promise to me. Somehow I knew God's word was true and He would take care of me and my small family.

When Lisa was about eight months old she started to get extremely ill and would frequently have to be hospitalized. She seemed to be allergic to almost everything that came her way; dust, mold, feathers, dogs, and cats. We lived on the Mississippi River where mold counts are always high in the air, so that was one count against her. My first thought was to get her away from the damp, mold infested air. I was amazed at how quickly the Lord found me an apartment in a good area in Iowa. We were blessed to find this little church not far from where we lived so I was able to walk to the church with the children in tow. My new church family inspired and helped keep my spirits up through many difficult times. I was able to clean the church and make a little extra money to subsidize my income which was in extreme need. The state stepped in and helped with food stamps and the medical benefits I desperately needed with Lisa being so ill.

Lisa became so sick that she was in the hospital more than she was home. She was a premature baby and the doctors had warned me to expect she might not be as healthy in her first few years. However, I was not prepared for such a sick child after James was so happy and healthy. The hospital Lisa was in was far from our home and I did not have the income to drive daily so I would walk. It was still winter in Iowa so many days it was a bitter walk. The pastor and his wife were God sent, offering to help watch James when I would go to the hospital.

I knew this couldn't go on though, and that I had to acquire a place closer to the hospital. I watched the paper for weeks, but that was a desirable area to live in and it seemed no one wanted to move out once they were there. I prayed hard daily for something to open up so I could be close to the hospital and my sick little daughter. One day I found an apartment listed in the paper.

I drove over for an interview at the landlord's house. I could tell when I met the lady who was renting the apartment that she was a Christian. One can tell those things when you can see the light shining through them. I thought for sure this was the place for me and my children. What a blessing it was going to be.

As the lady stood and looked at me, I can imagine what she must have thought when she saw how young I was and with two small children. She explained they didn't rent to anyone who had children, it was an upstairs apartment, and she thought I could find something more suitable. I was in shock as I stood there. I had been so certain this was the answer to my prayers. I started crying.

"Oh please," I explained, "my daughter is so ill and I have to be next to the hospital for her, she is there so much. I prayed so hard for this apartment and please, please reconsider."

Thinking the she didn't understand how much I needed it, I told her I was a very responsible young lady who had fallen on hard times and needed her help. By that time I was almost on my knees pleading for her to reconsider. She was crying also and told me to wait outside for a minute while she discussed it with her husband. It seemed forever, but I'm sure it was only ten minutes or so. She came out and informed me she would rent it on certain conditions. They wanted it to stay clean and she wanted to be able to come in anytime and check on the apartment. I was so elated I reached out, hugged her, and told her she was welcome in my home anytime she wished. I told her of Lisa's allergy to dust and how everything in my home had to be dust proofed, so it would always be clean enough for her to come and eat off my floors.

After we'd lived in the apartment for with a short while, I went downstairs to check the mail and the door closed and locked behind me. I was frantic! Our landlords lived down the street on the next block. I ran down the street as if I was a crazy woman banging on her door. Thank goodness she was home. I explained the situation, she reassured me all would be okay and came back and let me in. She used the opportunity to check on the apartment and was very pleased about the cleanliness. I offered her cookies and coffee or tea. I was so happy to be safe with my children, but she chuckled and declined. This was the only time in a year she ever came into my home although I certainly offered her coffee and cookies anytime she would like. God had blessed me greatly and I knew He was taking care of my family and me.

Thank goodness we had the apartment within a block of the hospital because Lisa continued to get sick more often. It seemed I was in the hospital with her more than I was home. My Aunt HaHa came to take James for weeks at times while I was constantly with Lisa in the hospital. What a blessing my aunt and uncle have been all my life. They lived about an hour away from where I was, but I knew James was safe and loved in their hands.

One time when Lisa got very sick, the doctors gave her penicillin. She turned beet red all over and her temperature raged. The nurses told me she would be fine, but a mother can sense when the doctors are fearful. I thought for sure I was going to lose my baby that time, but God prevailed. Our days and nights ran into each other at times. For days I would stay holding my daughter's small fragile hand so she could suck her thumb and sleep. They had her tied down like a small animal with IVs in both legs and her other hand tied so she couldn't try to pull out the IVs. She was so ill she hardly ever made a sound other than to cry if she couldn't suck her thumb. It was one of the hardest times in my life; knowing only God could save my child. There was not one thing I could do other than pray. I have certainly spent a lot of time in my life on my knees praying for God to intercede on my behalf.

The nurses and doctors all knew me by name and they got together and purchased me a rocker to sit in next to Lisa on her long stays at the hospital. I think they were caring for me also. When I think back there were times when they would say, "Mary, you have to go home and get cleaned up and get a couple hours rest." They were such a blessing at that great time of need.

Finally, I was informed by the doctors that Lisa wouldn't make it through her next stay at the hospital. She was too frail and fragile to handle another bout with a sickness. They suggested I take her as quickly as I could to Arizona so the dry heat could dry out her lungs. Once again the Lord had been working in advance on our behalf. My sister and her family had moved to Arizona a couple years earlier and were able to sponsor us for a while.

Lisa did get well, she had a difficult time with her allergies and asthma growing up, but I am happy to tell she is a RN now and takes care of others. I know anyone receiving from her will have excellent care.

So when I was in O'Hare airport and I saw this young lady with her family trying to find their way, I reached out and helped. I explained how much I was blessed by so many people God had sent my way when I was much like her. I knew she would pass it forward later. A kind word and a smile go so far, do not cost a thing, but are worth more than silver and gold. I hope you are able to reach out and help someone else that is going through the same thing you did. Remember where we came from and how far the Lord has taken us and be compassionate. We all have burdens we bear, let's help lighten the loads of others and allow the light of Jesus to shine through us.

Thoughts to Ponder

Take a moment and think about all the people who have been a special blessing in your life. Pause from your busy schedule and say a special prayer for them, and thank God that He sent them to you right when you needed them. Then ask the Lord to open your eyes to see those around you that could benefit from your help. Be willing to give back out of what you have so generously received from God. You will be amazed at what a smile and a kind word can do. Be ready and willing to do whatever the Lord directs and you will not only be a blessing to others, you will be blessed beyond measure.

Pray: *Father God, thank You for sending those special people into my life right when I needed them. Thank You for showing me just how much You care for me, and how You are always watching over me and my loved ones. Help me to now bless others as they have blessed me.*

Chapter 11

MICHELLE ANNIE

Giving is part of the "planting seed and harvest" principle which God placed in order when He made this amazing earth for us to live in. It is a proven fact that when you give, it is not just the one who receives the gift that is blessed, you also receive a blessing. This is a story of how the Holy Spirit led me through a test of my obedience in this area of giving where I feel I received more than the one who accepted the gift. God truly does reward us for our willingly obedient hearts.

Texas was windier than I had anticipated when I moved from Illinois. Managing big stables had always been one of my childhood dreams. I was now living in Texas where I was managing and training horses. We'd had a good year with the horses and they had placed high in the competition shows. Because of this several horses were going on to the All Arabian Regional Horse Show in Dallas. A couple days before the Arabian Regional in Dallas, I met a new client. Mae brought in a couple horses for me to train while I was in the middle of grooming horses for the show, which included body clipping to make them fresh and clean looking. Mae was a delightful woman that had kind eyes and a smile that made me smile. You could see she had some special gifts, but on this particular day I could not stop and appreciate those gifts. I was very busy.

I apologized to her saying time was something I didn't have plenty of that day so I would talk to her when I had an opportunity to properly access her horses. She told me if I needed any help while the majority of my staff was away at the show to just let her know and she would be happy to help. That did sink in my mind and I put her paper work on my desk. I would file it when all had settled down and I had a free moment.

A few days later all but one of my staff went with the horses to the Regional Show. My day was going exceptionally well. All the horses had been out for their exercise and it was time to bring them in and start with the afternoon feeding. One of the yearling colts was left in the arena. When I was about to bring him in he turned and kicked me with both back feet, breaking several of my ribs, my sternum, and putting some ribs through my lung.

I won't go into all the details, but I remembered what Mae had said about coming to help. Her paperwork was still on my desk. When I finally was able to get to the office, I called the ambulance. They were on their way, but I felt I needed to call Mae.

I phoned her and somehow she knew who I was when all I could say was, "I need help."

She was like Atlas Woman. She was there before the ambulance and she lived twice as far away. By then I didn't have enough oxygen to even answer the questions the paramedics were asking. Mae tried her best to answer them for me, but she didn't even know my last name. We had just met for a couple minutes when she dropped her horses off. I had planned to contact her after I had all the horses off to the show, but had not yet had the opportunity. This was certainly not what I had in mind for my call to her.

Mae rode in the ambulance with me, stayed at the hospital until I was all settled in, and then called her husband to come and get her. The doctors recognized me when I showed up at the hospital because I had many of their horses in training. It was funny because the doctors were all coming in asking if it was their horse that had kicked me. All I could do was shake my head indicating no it was not any of the doctor's horses. I just wanted to be treated for the pain and have them make it so I could breathe. Of course I was admitted to the hospital.

My children were in high school and Mae tried to make sure that all was taken care of at home. I was blessed. James, my son spoke Spanish well enough to communicate with the staff member that witnessed the whole thing. James also knew how to take care of the horses and feed them. Each horse had his own menu and it was posted on the front of each stall. That one farm hand and James took care of everything until I was able to get out of the hospital. I wanted to get home as soon as possible even though the doctors didn't want me to leave. I was a concerned single parent with two teenage children at home by themselves.

I must have been out of my mind from the pain meds to come home though, because the pain was nearly unbearable. I had to have pain shots through my ribs into the pain centers so I could walk and breathe at the same time. Not a great time in my life, but I did get to know Mae, this wonderful godly woman and her husband who changed my life. They took us into their home and helped care for me until I was able to get back on my feet to work the horses.

While I spent some time with Mae I came to the understanding she was a bit fearful of the horses. She did a good job handling them but she never rode. She'd had a bad experience while she was on a horse and she couldn't gather the courage to get back on. Sometimes that is a good thing, but in her case she was a good horse person, the horses trusted her, and she was a natural handler. She was missing out on the wonderful experience of riding. You and the horse become as one, and the world goes by with no problems while you're riding. It is an experience like nothing else.

I had a special mare, Michelle Annie, that had been abused by her previous owner and it had taken me over a year working with her before she wouldn't almost collapse when a man walked into the barn. I had decided that she would be my horse and that her life would end with me. I would keep her until she died. Michelle Annie had never given me any trouble training her. She had a great mind after she conquered her fears and learned to trust me. This was just the kind of horse that Mae needed to get her passed her fear of riding.

One day I felt the Lord was telling me to give Michelle Annie to Mae. I thought that couldn't be what He was telling me. Michelle Annie was safe where I could protect her, but the feeling wouldn't leave me. One thing I have learned from all the things God has taken me through is that I only need to be obedient and He will take care of all my needs.

So I gathered Michelle Annie's Arabian Registry papers and took them to Mae. Mae couldn't believe I was giving her one of my best horses and especially this mare. Mae had many horses and it would take her most of the day just feeding them. She also had Barbados sheep, turkeys, chickens, and on and on. It was truly Old McDonald's farm. Mae loved her ranch and you could feel the peace when you drove down the lane. It was a great feeling. You knew you would be treated like family in her home. This special couple had no children of their own, though I know God blessed them with all that came and spent time with them. They made so many of us part of their extended family.

Being obedient to the Lord is always the right thing to do. He always has the best for us even when we can't see it. It's like we are part of this big puzzle and when our pieces don't touch the other pieces we think they don't have any connection to us, which of course is not the truth. We all belong on the puzzle and the picture is not complete unless we are all connected correctly.

After Mae had been riding Michelle Annie all over the ranch for about six months and looking like she had the tiger by the tail, she came up to me with the mare's registry papers. She said the Lord knew how much it took for me to be obedient and to give that horse to her to help her. This had given Mae the healing she needed and also stretched my faith. Isn't God great to fix two birds with one stone or should I say one horse! I told her that I'd love to have Michelle Annie back, but only if she was sure and that she would promise to keep riding. Michelle Annie was happy to come home and I was excited to have her back, thanking God for giving me the desires of my heart.

But the natural man receiveth not the things of the Spirit of God: for they are foolishness unto him: neither can he know them, because they are spiritually discerned. (1 Corinthians 2:14)

In the natural we have to be quiet enough in our lives to hear what the Lord is trying to tell us. We can't afford to miss this gift of the Holy Spirit that we are given when we accept Christ Jesus as our Lord. The Lord can help us out of trouble if we are willing to listen and have faith.

Listen to that small still voice that you hear whisper in your spirit just for a few seconds. If you don't respond, it will go away as Satan tries to steal away the thought. Act quickly and learn to cultivate this wonderful gift of the voice of the Holy Spirit talking to you.

Many times it seems the things God tells us don't line up with what our natural mind thinks. Our spirit is nobler than our minds so we need to learn to listen closely to the Lord. We need to stop being concerned with what others think and do what we know is the right thing. Our walk through this land is temporal; we should be concerned that we answer most of all to our Heavenly Father.

Thoughts to Ponder

Seek to be quiet enough to hear what the Lord is saying to you through His Holy Spirit. Learn to be immediately obedient to His voice, and realize He has only the best gifts for you. Your Heavenly Father knows the deepest desires of your heart and longs to give them to you. He just needs you to trust and obey Him.

Pray: *Thank You Heavenly Father that You always have my best interests at heart. Help me to listen and hear Your voice and to willingly obey the promptings of the Holy Spirit.*

Chapter 12

SPEAKING BLESSINGS

I t seems our society has forgotten how important it is to speak blessings over our children. I recently read a book written by a pastor that reminded me that in times past "blessings" were spoken over the children and they excelled in those areas in their lives.

This pastor shared that his mother had raised him by herself until he was fourteen years old, so this did not allow the luxury of a blessing from his father. Then his mother remarried and she was married to his stepfather for forty-eight years. Even through this long period of his mother's second marriage he did not receive a spoken blessing on his life. Only after his stepfather had passed away did he receive a blessing from a fellow pastor whom he respected. His life was changed by this one event.

And I will make of thee a great nation, and I will bless thee, and make thy name great; and thou shalt be a blessing. (Genesis 12:2)

This was God's word spoken to Abram, who later became Abraham and the father of great nations as the Lord had spoken over him.

In Genesis 27 it speaks of how the first blessing was an important issue. Isaac's age had taken his sight. When it came time for him to bless his sons who were twins, Jacob came in and tricked his father into giving him the first blessing which was due to his twin, Esau, who had come first at birth. It was a hardship for many years for Jacob who had stolen the birth right from his brother. This gives us insight into how important in biblical times it was for a first son to receive a blessing from his father.

We need to keep in mind that our children, sons and daughters included, need to know beyond a shadow of doubt, we love them and that we say prayers over them daily. Do we always like what they do? Certainly not and I'm sure there are times they are not happy with our actions either, but it does not change the fact we will always love them and continually pray over them.

The children in my life know without doubt I love them. They know I am going to pray for them daily, each and every one of them, including the nephew's we raised as our own. They all know I will speak blessings on them as well. If something goes haywire, they know they can call me or my husband and we will do what we feel is within our reach to help, without hindering or enabling.

I want to encourage you to bring your children to you. If they are where you cannot personally put your hands on them, call them. Take time and think seriously of how you would like to bless them and let them know how special they are to you and God. There is nothing like knowing someone has the best intent for you, and they will always be praying and speaking blessing over you.

We see in the Bible how the father, the head of the household, took the first son and blessed him. There were circumstances where it took almost a lifetime for the blessings spoken over them by their fathers to come about, such as when Jacob spoke blessings over Joseph (Genesis 49:22-26). In

Genesis 49:1-28, blessings were spoken for each of Jacob's sons, all of which can be traced through Israel's rocky history. Joseph was a favorite of his father because Jacob was so in love with Rachel, Joseph's mother, and so he was shown special favor. Of course this did create strife between the other brothers who had different mothers. Joseph told of the dreams where he felt God had shown him he was going to rule over the other brothers and the jealousy ran wild. The jealousy became so bad that Joseph was sold into bondage by his own brothers and his father took him as dead. The blessing spoken over Joseph in Genesis 49:22-26 came after they were re-united many years later in Egypt.

I have noticed it seems hard for a person to rise above the ruler or standard they feel others have placed on them. Why does this happen? We listen to what others say and forget what God says about us and how God sees us, and give credence to what others speak. If we could remember the Lord reminds us to do unto others like we would like to have done to us, this would make life a bit easier (see Matthew 7:12). We would speak words of encouragement and affirmation of how God sees us, and it would be easier to rise above the hindrances of this world.

Have you ever seen someone walk into the room and it seems to light up and the party is on? Yet on the other hand we see people walk into the room and a damper is placed on the room and it seems the party is over? Why is that? Do others see us as we see ourselves, possibly? Don't we sense when someone is looking at us and turn to see them turn away. How many times has your spouse, if you are married, been looking at you and you know what they are thinking?

Our thoughts and intentions for other people seem to be sent out in the universe even though they are not spoken. How many times has this happened to you? Maybe more than you can count I would think. Even babies, when they look at us bring our attention to them, and look at how small they are, yet we are affected by their thoughts. This shows just how important it is to give our children hugs and touch our spouses in a loving manner. I remind my husband every day I pray for wisdom for him and the knowledge to use it. I pray Warrior Angels around him to protect him.

One day my husband came home from work with a strange look on his face. We happened to have company staying with us at the time and they started talking to him as he came into the room. Instantly I knew something was amiss. I asked him what's up, and he told me I wasn't going to believe it and turned pale. My husband has a light complexion anyway, so I told him to sit down. He pointed to his new cowboy boots. One had a large hole right through the top of the toe of his boot.

He explained to me that he and another man were moving a motor and it slipped out of their hands, ran down his leg, across his knees, and landed right on his foot. He had a large red line that ran down his leg as I saw later. It was truly a miracle he had a knee left. The motor had a protruded end that had punched through the top of his boot. He explained he'd been fearful of taking his boot off when the men were able to get the motor off his foot because he could not feel his foot or toes. They should have been sheared off, but by the grace of God, the sharp protrusion of the motor had pierced through his boot right between his big toe and the toe next to it. His toes were very sore and red but not broken! God's angels had spared my husband's leg, knee, toes, and foot! Our friends and the people that were around my husband that day kept saying that it was nothing short of a miracle.

The next day my husband was about to leave and came to give me for my customary kiss and hug before leaving. He stood and continued to look at me and I could see he needed more than I was giving him.

I asked, "What?"

He continued to look at me and I asked, "Do you want me to say an extra prayer over you today?"

He answered, "It wouldn't hurt; I'm heading off for work again."

Even though my husband knew I prayed for his safety every day and blessings on him daily, he needed to be reassured as many of us do. Take the time to let your loved ones know you pray safety and blessings for them daily. By all means do pray these things over them, they are so important! We need to place the angels in working order. Think how many angels are waiting for you to speak them into work on your behalf to cover and bless your loved ones.

The Bible says what we speak here on the earth will be loosed in heaven. Speak up and let your request be known. Speak those blessings on your loved ones and let them know you are speaking a prayer on them daily.

Thoughts to Ponder

It seems our society has forgotten how important it is to speak blessings over our children. We need to keep in mind that our children, sons and daughters included, need to know beyond a shadow of doubt, we love them and that we say prayers over them daily. I want to encourage you to bring your children to you. Think seriously of how you would like to bless them and let them know how special they are to you and God. There is nothing like knowing someone has the best intent for you, and they will always be praying and speaking blessing over you.

Beware that you do not despise or feel scornful toward or think little of one of these little ones, for I tell you that in heaven their angels always are in the presence of and look upon the face of My Father Who is in heaven. (Matthew 18:10 AMP)

The Bible says what we speak here on the earth will be loosed in heaven (Matthew 16:19). Speak up and let your request be known. Speak those blessings on your loved ones and let them know you are speaking a prayer on them daily.

The Angel of the Lord encamps around those who fear Him [who revere and worship Him with awe] and each of them He delivers. (Psalm 34:7 AMP)

Pray: *Thank You, heavenly Father that You bless us as Your beloved children. Thank You for the example You have given us to also speak blessings over our children. We thank You for Your ministering angels that go out and protect our loved ones as we pray for their protection and favor daily.*

Chapter 13

ARE WE LIKE GRASS?

eople ask me, "You don't worry about what other people
think about you, do you?"

The answer is, "No, I don't have to answer to people. I'm
concerned about answering to God when my time is through,
and how He could sit me down if I don't listen to Him."

I hate to admit it, but I have had that happen and it is not
a pretty sight when God sits you down to have time out! As I
was reading scriptures, this one came to me and I felt it was
the scripture to inspire me as I seek to focus on obeying the
Lord and not what others might think of me.

*I, even I, am He who comforts you. Who are you
that you fear mortal men, the sons of men, who are
but grass, that you forget the Lord your Maker, Who
stretched out the heavens and laid the foundations of
the earth, that you live in constant terror every day
because of the wrath of the oppressor, who is bent on
destruction?* (Isaiah 51:12-13 NIV)

When we break this scripture down it is amazing. Let's
start with God telling us He is the one who comforts us. Nice
way to start a lesson like we do our children. We comfort

them first and then explain what we want them to learn and understand. Second, He asks us who we really think we are to fear mortal men who are like grass. When I read this it hit me that grass and men find their "roots" in the dust. Grass grows in the dirt and God gathered dirt and blew life into us making us human. When we think about it we do expire quickly in the scheme of things. Maybe this is God's way of reminding us in our realm of time the grass expires as quickly as our lives do to Him: a possible comparison.

Third, He reminds us that we have forgotten our Maker and Lord who created the heavens and earth if we are living in fear of man. He asks why we would put our focus on someone who would like to destroy us instead of keeping our eyes on Him, who loves us and created us. If we read further in the chapter to Isaiah 51:16 it says, "and (God) covered you with the shadow of My hand" (NIV). When He holds us in His hand we know nothing is able to pluck us out. When all is said and done we see from God's Word we have nothing to fear.

For God has not given us the Spirit of Fear; but of power, and of love, and of a sound mind. (2 Timothy 1:7)

The Word says God has not given us the Spirit of Fear! When we realize that it is a spirit that Satan sends to get us off stride with what God has for us to be blessed, we can take charge and command that evil spirit to go as Jesus did. God has given us a sound mind, not one of fear and indecision that allows us to be whipped this way and that in the wind as the grass sways in the wind.

If we are to truly come to God like children, we need to realize our natural children aren't fearful when their father is around. Children know without a doubt their father would never allow someone to hurt them. That is why children are

80

fearless, as they say, and that is what God wants us to be like! Fearless!

So do I get fearful about what people are going to think of me? No! I know that I reside in my Father's hand, and God will fight the battles for me. All I have to do is be obedient and love the Lord with all my heart, soul, and mind and He will take care of the rest. He has already sent His only begotten Son, Jesus Christ for my salvation and with that my sin is taken away and my health has been restored. Allow God to be your father and stop worrying about the things that will probably never happen. Understand that it is a spirit of fear that comes to you, tries to trick you, and does not line up with what God's blessings are.

Here is an acronym for fear that you need to keep before you daily so you will not be tempted to allow it to rule your life.

F.E.A.R. = False Evidence Appearing Real

In Psalm 23 it says, "Though I walk through the valley of the **shadow** of death..." (NKJV). It does not say through the Valley of Death. Do you see it? It is only a shadow. We don't have to be scared of the things of this world that are just shadows. Shadows tend to make things appear greater than they are. Hold on to our Lord and Savior, that is what is eternal and **will not** be gone like the grass which withers away.

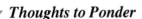

Thoughts to Ponder

Why do you get concerned about what someone else thinks?

How do you feel knowing that fear is not from God?

Can you see that God is your true comfort and you can live in the assurance of His love?

Pray: *Thank You Father God that You are my comfort and the source of my security. Help me to remember every day that I need not fear what man might say or do to me. Thank You that You have offered me eternal life through Your Son Jesus Christ.*

Chapter 14

PUMPKIN SEED

W e had been in foster homes for a couple years before Grandma and Grandpa were able to get us after our mother had been hospitalized. School was letting out for the summer so we had an opportunity to get more familiar with our grandparents before dealing with entering a new school. That summer we learned to trust our Grandparents and our new surroundings. Our time in foster care had taught us not to trust anyone. We now had to learn not everyone was out to hurt us. Trust is something earned, not something given freely. We had learned that lesson very young. Our Grandparents had brought us to safety and we began to feel blessed to be able to reside with them.

Our Grandparents were also taking care of our mother because she had just been released from the extended care hospital due to a grand mall seizure which had left her in a coma and totally incapacitated. Mother was learning how to pick up buttons and her speech was still far from perfect when we first saw her after arriving at our Grandparents' home.

As the summer progressed, we learned to play games we'd never heard of and we grew to depend on and love our Grandparents. I could only remember having seen them a couple times before because of the demands of farm life and the fact that we lived out of state. Running a farm like theirs didn't leave much time to venture out to another state for the day. Cows needed to be milked, pigs slopped, chickens fed, and the list goes on and on. They also raised their own crops that needed constant attention. We had a lot to learn about life on a farm.

When the new school year began, we were able to attend LaGrange Elementary School. Things had settled down and the fall festival at the school was just around the bend. Grandmother decided to dress us all in Halloween garb. She was quite the seamstress. She could even make a pattern from something you had on. She would lay it on the floor and just cut out a pattern and duplicate it.

Grandma miraculously designed a costume for each of us in a day or so. I don't remember what everyone else was dressed as, but I do remember I was dressed up as a pumpkin. She even made it orange and stuffed me with some kind of stuffing so I was very round and my arms stood straight out due to the stuffing. Needless to say I was not very happy with this big orange costume I was placed in though no one else seemed to be concerned with their costume. The day of the harvest party arrived and off we went to the LaGrange Elementary School.

The school was packed with children and adults. In many cases you couldn't tell who they were due to the face masks. I didn't have a face mask, but my green collar kept lifting and getting in my face. I had to keep pushing it down in order to not only see where I was going but breathe properly. I stood close to my Grandmother. My sister, whom I normally stuck to like glue, had disappeared into the crowd as soon as we entered the building. She loved parties like this, but I didn't like being surrounded by so many people. I felt totally out of my element, so I clung to my Grandparents.

Soon I was instructed to run off and play with the other children and enjoy this great party while the adults talked.

I was directed to a haunted house which was built inside the school. I complained the whole time trying to hang onto Grandmother's arm, but I was pried loose and shoved through the door of the haunted house. The door closed behind me. As my eyes tried to adjust to the darkness, a man with a bloody knife and a screaming man that had been stabbed tried to grab me. When their hands touched me, I began screaming at the top of my lungs, scratching, kicking, and biting in all directions. I begged them to let me back out, but they told me I had to travel on through the maze of horrors to get to the exit. I let them know in no uncertain terms I was not going any further into this horrible place!

Finally I won and backed out the same door I'd entered still screaming and crying. Of course my Grandmother came to my aid. The hysteria was so bad she actually held me. I felt bad that I was so terrified, but I couldn't stop crying. I have not gone back to any haunted houses since and it is certainly not on my bucket list of things to do.

However, as I have grown up and had children of my own, I realize that unfamiliar things can have similar effects on us. When my children would get fearful of something, I was quick to reach out, hold and comfort them, even when I could see the thing they were fearful of was not going to hurt them.

We get fearful even as adults, and many times it is only shadows that our imagination has created. We can understand how as children things new and undiscovered make them fearful. We need to seek to understand the cause of our fear and take it to our true Comforter who will help us deal with it.

2 Timothy 1:7 says, "For God has not given us a spirit of fear, but of power and of love and of a sound mind" (NKJV).

 ### Thoughts to Ponder

Though fear is real to us when we experience it, Jesus said in John 14:16, "And I will

85

pray the Father, and he shall give you another Comforter, that he may abide with you forever." Just like we do not want our children to live in fear, God our Heavenly Father wants us to feel secure in our relationship with Him. He has given us His Holy Spirit to comfort us and assures us of His love for us. 1 John 4:18 says, "There is no fear in love; but perfect love casts out fear" (NKJV). God's love for us is perfect, unconditional, and forever!

Pray: *Thank You Father God for Your love. Help me to understand Your love and to rest secure and free from the spirit of fear in Your loving care.*

Chapter 15

PIGEONS

One morning my friend Chrystal came into the shop extremely upset. She told me what a terrible person she was and what had happened that morning.

Her plight started earlier that day when Chrystal was out in her front yard weeding around her bushes. Chrystal is a bit of a perfectionist and as she was stooped over reaching under her bushes, she threw out a couple rocks that did not match the colored landscaped stones. In Arizona many yards are decorated with colored rocks instead of grasses due to the cost of water. The heat here has a tendency to cook everything in its path especially when it hits 100 degrees or more.

She heard a bird rustle out from under the bush that startled her a bit, but she continued to weed and toss out the unmatched stones. A strange squawk sounded from behind her and as she turned she saw a pigeon that had apparently been stuck by one of the stones she had tossed behind her. This bird was in distress, stumbling around like a Weeble Wobble Toy. Chrystal was shocked to think she had struck and hurt this poor bird that apparently had been hiding under her bushes.

She has a tender heart for animals and ran into the house to ask her husband what in the world she could do to relieve this poor bird. Her husband reassured her that in no time at all the bird would shake it off. He was sure it would be fine. Chrystal got busy in the house doing things for the day and forgot about the bird, trusting in the advice of her loving husband.

Later in the day as she glanced out the window, she noticed women were gathering in a circle across the street from her house and decided to investigate. When she crossed the street she noticed they were looking down at this pigeon and was discussing what kind of disease this bird may have to be wobbling around in erratic circles.

Chrystal noticed it was the same bird she had "stoned" that morning while working in her yard. It was obvious this bird was still not quite right. She didn't want to tell the ladies she had struck the bird earlier in the day without meaning to, but in her dilemma she wondered what she should do. Some commented maybe they should put the poor bird out of its misery. Others thought it could be diseased and maybe they should call someone to come and get it checked. The list of suggestions went on and on. Chrystal was silent just covering her mouth wondering what in the world to do. None of the options seemed very humane to her especially as she felt responsible for the little bird's current condition.

In an instant the decision was taken out of their hands when a giant owl swooped down from out of nowhere and grabbed up this sad looking injured pigeon. It was all over. The women were in shock and Chrystal did not have to divulge what had happened earlier in the morning. As she told me the story almost in tears, I couldn't help but laugh. I know it wasn't the right thing to do, but everyone in the shop was laughing over this sad story.

When one thinks about it and puts it into perspective, it shows us just how much of life is out of our control around us. The ladies knew the little bird needed help, but were at a loss what to do for it. Yet God put an end to this poor bird's suffering in a merciful even productive way so that it did not have to be struck by something, discarded as trash or probed by a doctor. God had mercy on this little bird and on Chrystal who was suffering over the thought she had hurt one of God's creatures.

Jesus said in Matthew 10:29-31 that not one sparrow falls to the ground that the Father does not know about, and that we are more valuable to God than the sparrows so we need not live in fear.

How fast our live can come to an end. Maybe we aren't a bird, but I'm sure when he arose that morning looking for bugs and worms he was not thinking it would be his last day on earth. We know it can be ours as well, but we also know we have a God that has paid the price through our Savior, Jesus so we can join Him in heaven when He sends the great bird to take us home.

Thoughts to Ponder

Are you ready for our Lord to call you home? How does this story touch your life? Why do we think we can add one minute more of time when our God calls us?

Do you try to be in control of every situation?

Isn't it time you realize God has you in His hand and He has a better life for you then you can imagine?

Read Matthew 10:29-32 and then confess Jesus as your Lord and Savior this very day.

Pray: *Thank You Father God that You love me so much You sent Your Son Jesus to pay the price for me so I can come to heaven when my time here on the earth is done.*

Chapter 16

UNLIKELY EVENTS

When things happen to us and there seems to be no rhyme or reason for it happening, what is our response? Do we look for the answer and try to figure out what in the world just happened to us? Or do we take it in stride and think things just happen? Our life is full of these seemingly unexplained circumstances that happen almost daily to us if we really take the time to grasp them.

What is the driving force that causes these things to happen? How are we inspired to step out and do something out of our normal realm? What gives us the ability to reach beyond ourselves and touch another's life? What kind of circumstance or events does this set in order? These are all things that could show us how God is trying to keep us safe and bless us through the unlikely events in our every day lives.

God sends His angels daily to keep you safe as you drive in your car. I know you all have been amazed at how if you had not been late, you would have been in the accident that happened just moments before you arrived on that stretch of road. Think of all the times a child is barely missed by an automobile and you have thanked God for keeping that child safe. The list goes on and on as we take a few minutes and see what our responses are to these unlikely events.

I was working on a lady's hair in my salon and we were talking about unusual things that happen and why we find ourselves in these situations. She is a very timid and reserved lady, but decided to share how an unusual experience happened where she could see God's hand in the situation after she had the ability to look back in time.

Barb had recently lost her husband and her life was feeling a bit out of control with all the changes that came with her loss. She had decided to move to another state and downsizing was a must. This meant she would have to sort through all the possessions acquired over their many years together. Her husband was a bit of a gatherer, if you know what I mean. He was a collector of things, and the task seemed to be overwhelming.

Among all the furniture they had acquired they had one of the older organs. It was a beautiful piece of furniture, and over the years they'd both enjoyed playing it. She felt it would be easy to find a home for this wonderful piece they had come to love. She thought she would give it to one of the churches thinking surely they would be blessed. One call after another found no one wanted this older organ. They had all gone to the smaller organs and keyboards which were easier to be worked on. No one seemed to want this large precious organ that she and her husband had treasured.

As the days of sorting of other things in the home went by, her mind kept coming back to what to do with the bulky organ? It began to be on her mind morning, evening, and night. It kept her from a restful night's sleep so she started praying about what she would do with it. It got to the point it was on her mind constantly and worry started to creep up on her over the situation.

One day as she was taking a walk, a man pulled into his driveway down the street. She had seen him a few times in the past but had never met him or his wife. She was a reserved person and would never go and speak to a stranger, let alone come up and introduce herself, but that is exactly what she felt led to do. Barb said it felt natural to walk up to this stranger and ask if he would like to have an organ.

She said later she was in shock that she would stroll up and talk to a complete stranger. Her children were in shock over her uncommon behavior. What kind of person would just walk up to anyone and ask if they wanted an organ? Yet it felt like it was the correct thing to do at the time.

When Barb introduced herself to the man and asked if he would like to have an organ, the man told her he didn't know, but they could go into their home and ask his wife if she would like to have one. She casually walked in the home with the man and soon found that they were missionaries and were home schooling their children. Here she was in this family's home whom she had never even met before.

As she spoke with these strangers, she found the children enjoyed reading. Barb had a good library and expressed to their parents the children may enjoy some of her books as well. They started a friendship that became precious to Barb as she walked through that difficult time in her life. The family did come and take the organ and the children enjoyed visiting Barb and were blessed with several of her books.

Our discussion came around to why she felt so comfortable that day walking up to a stranger. Any other day in her life that would never have happened. What does make us do things that feel right at the time? I told her I felt it was our angels that guide us and the Holy Spirit that comforts us when we are out of our comfort zone (John 16:13).

Behold, I send an Angel before thee, to keep thee in the way , and to bring thee into the place which I have prepared. (Exodus 23:20)

For he shall give his Angels charge over thee, to keep thee in all thy way. They shall bear thee up in

their hands, lest thou dash thy foot against a stone.
(Psalm 91:11-12)

Barb felt it was just a fluke at first, but the more she thought about it and her family discussed it with her, they could see it was not just a coincidence that she happened to be walking down the street at the very same time the man pulled up and stepped out of his truck. She had been praying over the placement of the organ which had weighed heavy on her mind. She wanted someone to be blessed by it as she and her husband had been. God had found a way to bless His missionary family and answer Barb's dilemma at the same time. We know God never does something for just one purpose; He always does it for two or more. His ways are not our ways and they are much better!

How many times have we done something out of the norm and wondered why in the world did we do that? Then something miraculous happens to us because of our unusual response. How many times do we think about someone and it keeps bugging us as we can't stop thinking of them? When we call them they tell us they were about to call us or they had been thinking about us or maybe they were desperate to hear a friendly voice.

Years ago I felt the Lord was telling me to go and visit a friend of mine who lived way back in the mountains. Each time I went to visit her I got lost. One day I argued with the Holy Spirit about how it was getting late and if I went back in the mountains when it was about to be evening I might be stranded back there. What a terrible thing to argue with the Lord. I knew better and yet I talked myself out of going and doing what I felt weighed heavy on me. I did not go that day. I expressed to the Lord I would go in the next day or so.

The next morning I went to town and heard that my friend's husband had shot and killed himself. It was a bit later than the time when I felt the Holy Spirit was prodding me to go and visit her. My heart was broken and I had to ask her forgiveness. She told me it would not have made any difference, but I still wonder if that is the truth.

I no longer put it off when I feel led by the Lord to go, call, visit or whatever He tells me to do. I know many times we have to be willing to do what seems crazy or stupid, but it isn't crazy when we know God has a bigger plan than we have. The Lord says we are a peculiar people and we are certainly that; led by the Spirit not by our own minds.

We cannot be concerned about what others think of our actions when we know we are doing the will of God. Be **bold** and step out in faith. Faith is an action word. When we step out and act in faith, the Lord will show us the next step. It doesn't seem to appear until the first step has been made in faith. Just as in the action movies when the person cannot see where their next step will be and steps out anyway due to an undesirable effect of doom behind them. They step out in faith and the footing is there under their foot, even though it cannot be seen from their vantage point with the natural eyes. We too must step out when prompted by the Lord. He will provide the way; He will never send us where He cannot reach us.

Trust God, He will not let us fall as long as we keep our eyes on Him and don't get swayed by our surroundings. We are to keep our eyes on the solution not the problem. If we keep our eyes on the problems we will perish like the people who came out of Egypt and were smitten by the serpents. Moses made the staff with the snake on it for the people to keep their eyes on instead of their bites. When they kept their eyes on the staff they were healed which was a depiction of Christ on the Cross in the later times (Numbers 21:9).

Things to Ponder:

What do you feel controls these unusual experiences in your life?

When unexplained things happen to you what is your response?

Do you look for the answers when you see unexplained blessings?

When was the last time you stepped out of the box to do something out of the normal realm?

What gives you the ability to reach beyond yourself and touch another's life?

What kind of circumstance of events does this set in order?

Do you ask for the angels to protect you daily?

Do you ask the Holy Spirit to lead you each and every day?

As you seek to answer each of these questions in your own life, pray and ask for wisdom from above as God has promised to give generously in James 1:5.

Pray: *Father God, I thank You for giving me Your wisdom from above. You are a generous and loving Father who has blessed me with so many blessings. Help me to see Your hand in my everyday life and to be ready to do Your will even if it seems foolish at the time. Help me to see You in each of these unexpected events.*

Chapter 17

WATCH GOD'S HAND

I t had been a long weekend where my sister and I had been singing at several churches. One of the services was held by a pastor who was from the south. I always enjoyed hearing his preaching. He did not beat around the bush with his messages. He always used his own daily circumstances to reach out and touch others. It is very effective sharing a bit of you.

I felt good about our worship music that morning and could tell many were touched by our songs allowing the Holy Spirit to fill the church. But as I listened to this pastor speak; I knew God had sent me there for this sermon which he was sharing.

On the way home which was about four hours away, I was talking to the Lord about this sermon. What exactly was God trying to talk to me about? Amazed at how He so often ministers to me in such a personal way, I asked God how He was able to come directly to me and care about me so personally. I have had Him touch my life with many miracles, but I still at times find it impossible to comprehend that God could love me and continue to love me that much. Ever feel like you don't deserve the awesome grace and love God pours over you?

Behold, the eye of the Lord is upon them that fear Him, upon them that hope in His mercy. (Psalm 33:18)

Even though there were very few cars on the road, it seemed unusually slow traveling for a late Sunday afternoon. I noticed as I was searching for God's heart, the clouds seemed to have rolled in around the mountains making it very blustery in a matter of just a few minutes time. It felt strange to have the clouds roll over the sky right where I was driving.

Slowing down as those dark clouds moved in, I looked into the darkness and the clouds suddenly opened! It looked like God's eye staring down at me! I have to admit, it certainly got my attention. I almost ran off the road when I saw this "eye" staring at me through the clouds. My questions were quickly answered when I could feel the presence of the Lord. I think every hair on my body was standing up straight.

I had asked God how, even though He was so busy, He had time to stop and pay attention to my needs. What a crazy thing for me to ask; a person who had been to heaven two times and sent back the last time and told to be a Faith Builder? Yet I had asked and the Lord did have my attention! You can read more on my time in heaven in my book, "On Fire for God."

At that point God reminded me of the many times the angels and Jesus told us in the Bible not to be fearful. He pointed out to me that I had a hidden fear I had never dealt with. Do you have the spirit of fear that creeps up on you? I think we all do at times in our lives.

I had raised my two children by myself after my divorce at eighteen, and I was always concerned how I would care for them properly. How would I be able to afford to feed, clothe, and keep a roof over them and me? I had so many questions even though God had told me He would take care of me and my children. He reminded me that He cared for the widows and their children and at that time I was a widow in His eyes. All through the years God had been faithful and supplied, but I had allowed Satan to put that little nagging fearful thought in my mind.

Now that my children were grown, God once again fulfilled all He'd promised. He gave me a godly husband, but I wasn't letting him be the head of the household due to the deep seeded fear that was so neatly tucked away in the depths of my mind. Funny how fears try to hide just deep enough and far back enough that we almost think they are not really there. It takes guts to bring those fears into the light and deal with the root of the evil that has had a hold on us.

The only arguments my husband and I would have were about finances. Had he ever let me go hungry since we'd married? No, absolutely not! Had I gone without a house to live in? No, of course not! My husband was the provider God had sent for me to have and to hold as my wonderful spouse, yet that fear had been tucked away. I'm sure Adam didn't understand why I was always concerned about what we were doing with our finances. He was doing his job, why wasn't I doing mine? My job was to trust God to give Adam the wisdom and knowledge he would need to succeed.

Looking back, I discovered where this long stemmed fear came from. When we were children we lived in a house where the snow blew in on us in the middle of the winter because the roof wasn't finished. We were hungry and cold much of the time. This was most likely the reason for this crazy fear, but it was now time to put an end to that fear.

The voice of the Lord came to me as clearly as when I was in heaven. He said, "Today you make a choice to either do what I tell you and believe I will always have the best for you or you can continue to stay in fear and let it rule and ruin your marriage. Today is the day, choose!"

I asked the Lord how I could break the cycle and make sure I didn't fall into this pattern again, and He gave me instructions. I was to go by Costco on the way home and He would instruct me what to do.

When I was standing in Costco the Lord directed me to the jewelry counter and said, "See that watch Adam was admiring last month? You go over and purchase the watch which will put your faith into action. That will break the spirit of fear. I know if you truly believe Me, your Lord, you will make that purchase, and it will be the visual for you and your husband to remember your covenant with Me."

I even asked, "God is that really you? How do I know for sure that it is You asking me to spend this money on something frugal?"

He reassured me that the amount I had in my billfold would be just the right amount to pay for this watch! Wow! How does He do that? Of course it was exactly the amount. I didn't even realize I had that much in my billfold, but there it was as my heart was beating a million miles a minute. I've never spent that kind of money on anything, not even my guitars.

"Now," I asked the Lord, "how in the world am I going to explain this to Adam? He is always watching TV when I come in and really doesn't want to hear about my trip."

The Lord told me not to worry about that, He would take care of Adam. I had stepped out in faith and God would take care of Adam's business from now on. I wasn't the head of the household, God was first and then Adam whom God would instruct.

I have to admit as soon as I left that store with that very expensive watch, I felt free as if a weight had been lifted off of me. When I was about to open the door to the house, Adam came to the door and eagerly asked me about my trip! The Lord had indeed paved the way. I told Adam about my whole trip and he listened intently. When I pulled out the watch and he opened it, it still had the price on the bottom of the plain white box.

Adam almost threw the watch back in the box as he declared, "I can't accept a watch like that! You need to take that back!"

"Absolutely not," I responded, "That is what the Lord told me to do. I am sorry that I have not allowed and trusted you to be the head of this household even when God gave me the desires of my heart, which was you. I knew you were a godly man and a man who would look after this family. There is nothing sexier than a man that is willing to do that! This will be ours to look on when we need to be reminded that God will lead us through and that He will give you the wisdom to do the right thing. I am not going to worry about that anymore. I know God and you will take care of our family."

"What if I make a mistake?" Adam asked.

I told him, "It will be okay, God will pick us up and I will be there to stand by you."

I promised I would pray for him daily that warring angels would protect him and that God would give him the knowledge and the wisdom to use all God had given him.

"We will be okay as long as we pray about it first and remember to keep God in the middle of our marriage," I told him confidently.

Several years have passed and that expensive watch is there as a daily reminder that God has been faithful. Once in a while I hear that little voice of fear asking if I am willing to accept it again. The answer is absolutely not! I pick up that watch and thank God for freeing me from the fear that held me captive. I praise my Lord for guiding and protecting my husband and our family.

We do not need to accept the spirit of fear. We need to realize that it is just a spirit sent from the evil one to keep us from being blessed by the Lord. We have every right to command that spirit of fear to go in the name of Jesus and it has to flee.

Submit yourselves therefore to God. Resist the devil, and he will flee from you. (James 4:7)

Reach out for God's guidance and keep yourself lined up with the Word of God. It will give you peace no matter what "spirit of fear" the enemy tries to slip into your thinking.

Thoughts to Ponder

Do you have a fear from something in the past? What have you done to set yourself free through God's will?

How does God talk to you?

Can you see all the times God has interceded for you?

You do not need to accept the spirit of fear, realize that is just what it is, a spirit sent from the evil one to keep you from being blessed by the Lord. You have every right to command that spirit of fear to go in the name of Jesus and it has to flee. Reach out for God's guidance and keep yourself lined up with the Word of God, it will give you peace.

God is love. When we take up permanent residence in a life of love, we live in God and God lives in us. This way, love has the run of the house, becomes at home and mature in us, so that we're free of worry on Judgment Day—our standing in the world is identical with Christ's. There is no room in love for fear. Well-formed love banishes fear. Since fear is crippling, a fearful life—fear of death, fear of judgment—is one not yet fully formed in love. (1 John 4:17-18 The Message)

Pray: *Thank You Heavenly Father for Your love. Thank You that I do not have to live with the spirit of fear. I receive Your perfect love in my life right now and command that spirit of fear to leave me in the name of Jesus.*

Chapter 18

JOY OF THE WORD

W hen I was about five years old, I was fascinated with reading. My older siblings were in school and their excitement was catching as I saw them unfold other worlds through the books they read. We didn't have many books to read other than my sibling's school books, but every night our mother would read from her Bible. We would sit around listening intently about the awesome God who created this wonderful universe.

The words from the Bible seemed to jump out at me. I was taught with the King James Version, which is still my favorite translation. My spirit would leap with joy when mother would read to us. I knew beyond a shadow of doubt that Jesus was my Savior and the King of kings by the stories she would read. I could hear how much God loved us to create such a world of wonder. The thing I find exciting is God created all this for us and then created us. He is always amazing us with miraculous things in our lives. Each day I am touched by His Grace.

God spoke to me through the Bible even as a child. I was desperate to learn to read so God could speak to me personally without having someone else read to me. I wanted to be able to go and spend time alone with God; just Him and me on that personal level. My favorite thing still is spending time alone with Him when all is quiet in the house.

There are times in the middle of the night when I hear Him call to me, "Come and spend time with Me and open My Bible and read what I have to tell you."

I don't know how I would make it through day after day without God's Word preparing me for the amazing things He has for me, knowing of His grace and favor for me throughout each and every day.

Before I started school I had many of the foundational words memorized. I loved all the "thee's, thou's, and thou art's" that showed the promises of God for me and my family. The covenant God has made with us is mind boggling when we think every breath we take is a gift. I think that is why they call it the "present" time.

The God who made the world and everything in it is the Lord of heaven and earth and does not live in temples built by human hands. And He is not served by human hands as If He needed anything because He Himself gives all men life and breathe and everything else. (Acts 17; 24-25 NIV)

The Word of God says, "If you seek Him, He will be found by you" (1 Chronicles 28:9 NKJV). When we are willing to come to God with a heart to learn more about Him, He never hides himself (Matthew 7:7-8). He desires for us to know Him intimately. We were created to be dependent on Him (Matthew 6:33). He is our Father. It is written that we as parents know what is good for our children, how much more God as our Heavenly Father wishes to do good for us (Matthew 7:9-11).

Reading the Bible to our children and helping them to know God and know Jesus Christ as their personal Savior are the best gifts we can give our children. This investment in their lives is one that no money can measure. The Bible says, "Wisdom is much better than silver and gold" (Proverbs 16:16). Who do we think made the silver and gold? God, of course, and if we have an intimate relationship with our Lord, He will meet our needs and so much more. It is important that our children learn this crucial concept early in life.

If you are having trouble being consistent in your Bible reading, keep reading a little every day until you can't imagine going a day with having that time with God to lead you through your day. It's like the doctors tell people who don't like water to keep drinking it until your body says this is something it does like and needs. The Word of God is life sustaining just like natural water.

Ask your Lord and Savior to fill you up with it until you feel His Joy bubbling over within your soul. We can't live life to the fullest without our Maker involved in our lives. He made us and He knows what we need.

 ### *Thoughts to Ponder*

When did you realize God loves you?
Do you yearn to know Him better?
How do you feel God speaks to you?
Spend time reading His Word today and ask Him to show You just how much He loves and cares for you through His letters to you.

Pray: *Father God, thank You for Your Word that gives me Your life giving water to energize me each day.*

Chapter 19

GOD'S LOVE INTROVERTED

The plan of sowing / planting / reaping / harvesting was set up by God when He made creation. If you are a farmer you understand that when you plant a couple of seeds of corn, you have to wait with faith and anticipation that God is going to make that seed grow into an ear of corn that has many kernels. This is what the Bible calls sowing and reaping.

If you have ever planted anything such as corn you will notice when it does come up, you do not harvest peas from planting the few kernels of corn. You receive corn when you plant corn seed. Thank goodness we can rely on this planting and harvesting so we know what we need to plant to get the harvest we need and want.

Sowing money "seed" brings money back as your harvest. Sowing clothing into a ministry can bring you clothing in return as your harvest. I use this form of sowing and people bring me clothes that are like new for my harvest.

Do we sow expectantly? If we don't trust God's plan, we can miss our harvest and we have planted in vain. We need to know what God's plan is for us which means we need to spend time in His Word so we know what God wants and expects, and then sow seed that will bring us that harvest.

God's love is based on this same principle. God gives His love freely to us and we are to enjoy His love and then give love to others. When we take that seed of love that God has given us and we decide to keep it for ourselves and not to share that love with others, it becomes perverse. If we hold the love that God has given us too tightly it becomes a stumbling block for us. Soon our lives become detestable because we can only think of ourselves. We don't care what anyone else does as long as they don't upset our apple cart, as they say. "Don't make us mad and stay out of our way" is how we become. We refuse to love anyone else without conditions; and trust me, that is not love.

I know this from experience. When I was eight I was burned from my waist up with third degree burns. If you have ever seen a person that had major burns and they have no face and their ears are burned to nubbins that is how I looked. I resembled ground hamburger and no one, not even my family, as much as they loved me, could look at me.

Learning to accept who I was in Christ was a real walk of faith for me. Even though the Lord had let me return from heaven to come back, I felt anger and rejection for being left with burns. I had expected to return from heaven fully healed just as I was in heaven. If I had understood the realization of the request to return, I don't think I would have asked the Lord to allow me to come back.

Many people have similar tragedies and may have scars that don't show on the outside, but are just as painful on the inside. Learning to gather God's love as close as we can and share it with someone else is not always the easiest thing to do. Yet it is necessary to have a healthy relationship with our Father in Heaven and those around us.

Romans 13: 8 says, "Owe no man anything, but to love one another: for he that loveth another hath fulfilled the law."

Love is much like faith, the more we use it and share it with others the more it grows. If we don't use our faith we soon feel we have no faith, even though the Bible says the Lord has given us all the same measure of faith. We are the ones who have to plant and use the faith to make it grow, same as our love for others.

Romans 12:3 says, "For I say, through the grace given unto me, to every man that is among you, not to think of himself more highly than he ought to think: but to think soberly, according as **God hath dealt to every man the Measure of Faith**" (emphasis added).

If you will immerse yourself in the Bible and see how God loves and has made provisions for us over and over, you will see who you are in the Lord's eyes. It is a priceless lesson to learn and will carry you through life as you stay close to the Lord.

And to know the love of Christ, which passeth knowledge, that ye might be filled with all the fullness of God. Now unto him that is (our Source) able to do exceeding abundantly above all that we ask or think, according to the power that worketh in us. (Ephesians 3:19-20)

Spend time with Him daily and He will give you the grace and mercy to make it through each day. The Bible says not to worry about tomorrow for God's grace is sufficient of today. It's like rocking on a rocking horse, you never get anywhere, and you just get worn out. Usually the things that we worry about just wear us out and don't really happen. They are thoughts that should never be entertained in our minds.

Good thoughts are what the Lord tells us to dwell on daily. The things we dwell on are the things that happen. Once again we are planting seed in our hearts and minds. Let's make the harvest a great one!

Psalm 19:14 says, "Let the words of my mouth, and the meditation of my heart, be acceptable in Thy sight, O Lord, my strength, and my redeemer."

Thoughts to Ponder

Notice what you begin your day thinking about. Then observe what things happen during your day. When evening comes, evaluate the correlation between the thoughts you began with and the events that happened throughout your day. What have you learned about this concept of sowing and reaping?

Pray Psalm 19:14: *"Let the words of my mouth, and the meditation of my heart, be acceptable in Thy sight, O Lord, my strength, and my redeemer."*

Chapter 20

STRAIGHTEN UP

W hen I was born I had a club leg and Mother said I didn't walk until I was almost two years old. They tried to brace my leg to get it to straighten out. As I grew, one leg was still longer than the other and my knee still twisted into the other knee. As I walked my hips would shift. I learned to deal with it over the years.

My knee did hurt many times and as I trained horses my stirrup on the left side had to be two and a half inches shorter than the other stirrup. I would have my saddle laced so no one could change my stirrup setting. The judges at the horse shows always would call me to the center and tell me of my attire not being even. If you don't have a medical reason for it, you can be docked on points. After a few years the judges came to know me and they didn't bother me anymore.

Through the years I acquired injuries due to horse accidents and one that seemed to linger on was when I was tossed off a mare and broke my collar bone and tore my rotary cuff. I can remember seeing the top of the barn as my saddle leaked as they say. I had just been to a class on how to roll so you won't get hurt when you fall off. I had been tossed off horses for years so I don't know what made me think this class would help. Maybe it would have worked if I had just fallen off my horse, but I don't normally fall off a horse. They have to work a bit harder than that to get rid of me. I was catapulted off this horse high up into the air. I remember thinking, *This is really going to hurt when I land because I am so high that I can see the top of the barn.*

Funny when you are in an accident or something crazy happens, it seems to go on for eternity. You can think of so many things in a matter of seconds that it seems like minutes have passed. I even had time to think this would be a good time to try out this new roll. It didn't work well, though, as I landed on my shoulder a bit too much. I would have been better off landing flat and biting the dust, as they say.

It was months after this incident before I was able to handle the horses again. They set my collar bone wrong and didn't realize my rotor cuff was a mess until weeks after. I had to wear this brace which was not the proper one. Once again God blessed me with great friends that stepped up to help feed and handle the horses. I wasn't able to even do my own hair. You know that's bad when a woman can't bathe herself or do her own hair, especially when you are a cosmetologist; not good!

Finally, I was able to get into a specialist that started me on steroid shots in my shoulder to try to rectify the problem. I didn't want surgery when I was told I would be off work for at least another four months. That was not acceptable for my situation at that time. I never regained movement like I should have in that shoulder and there was daily pain. I was not able to reach farther back than straight down. That range of movement wasn't great, but I still could work and that was what counted.

Later in life I was studying on God's love and how He will come and walk with you through all the trials in your life. I felt led at this time to be in prayer for God to come and share with me the love I had experience when I was a child and in heaven. One thing I have noticed if you seek

God's face He is an honorable Father who wants that personal relationship with you.

For probably a month I was awaken in the middle of the night by my heavenly Father saying, "Come and spend time with Me, I have something wonderful to show you!"

I would wake up quickly, heat up the hot chocolate, gather up my Bible, and spend time with the Lord! Each and every night it was something new and stimulating. What a glorious time it is when the Lord wakes you and wants to spend time with you in a one-on-one relationship. I have placed some of the wonderful things God shared with me those nights in this book. I want you to know how His love and mercy is at our fingertips. How much more love can He give us? He already sent His only Son to die for each of us. What an awesome gift He has made available to us! We need to accept the gift as it was intended, and not try to work for it; that would not be a gift.

I had been studying about being in the healing realm and how you can receive a healing when you hear a *Rhema* word from God. *Rhema* is Greek and literally means an "utterance" or "thing said" from God. Matthew 4:4 says, "Man does not live by bread alone but on every **word (*Rhema*) that comes from God**" (NIV emphasis added).

I found the revelation of God's Word coming to me in all of His *agape* love and it was incredible. It was almost as if I was intoxicated by being in the presence of the Holy Spirit. I longed to be engrossed by His presence. I looked forward to going to bed to get a bit of rest before the Lord would wake me and ask me to share time with Him.

It is amazing how much time could pass while studying His Word. There were some nights it would be a couple hours, but it felt like just a few minutes had passed other than needing another cup of hot chocolate. Yet when I was able to go back to bed the Lord would allow me to be refreshed when I woke up in the morning. I was always excited to see what God had shown me for that day.

Early one morning the Lord woke me and I could feel His tangible presence like no other time and I heard Him ask me, "What do you want of Me?"

I asked Him, "What do You mean?"

Again He repeated the question, "What do you want of Me?" My mind was reeling trying to decide what I really wanted of God other than His love and to know He was touching my life daily. I thought of the healing *Rhema* Word of God and asked for a healing. I asked to have my club leg, which I had lived with for almost fifty years, to be made straight and to be the same length as the other leg. Then I asked for my rotary cuff not hurt, to be healed, and to have full range of movement so I could actually fasten my back strap without a struggle.

Suddenly I heard Him say to me, "So be it!"

I could hear my leg turning and stretching out. I thought for sure it was going to hurt with all the cracking and stretching, but it didn't hurt at all! My shoulder started cracking. I was already dancing remembering how Jesus had told everyone to do something to activate their faith. I started reaching up and swinging my arm around. I started shouting and praising God.

My knee is straight and my legs are the same length! I can reach behind my back to fasten my strap with no pain! The only thing I did not think about doing was to ask for my back and hips to be straightened. I had to learn to walk again and stand differently, but it is great to not have a club leg and to have range of movement in my arm! Needless to say I had to go to the chiropractor to get adjusted for a season. The doctor said that it was a miracle! He had not seen anything like it. What a witness for the healing power of God's *Rhema* Word! I told my doctor I didn't do anything but pray and trust God for my healing. God's incredible love met my needs and gave me the gift of healing.

The point is God's love is so incredible that He would send His only begotten Son to die for each of our sins. We don't have to clean up before we come to Him. As a matter of fact we can't clean up enough to stand before the Lord on our own, no matter what a great person we are. Our works do not get us into heaven. It is God's love that makes that available to each and every one of us, no matter who we are or what we have done in our lives.

For by grace are ye saved through faith; and that not of yourselves; It is the gift of God. Not of works, lest any man should boast. (Ephesians 2:8-9)

The time that we spend in His Word helps us to know our Lord personally and that is the walk I want. I challenge you to step out and ask the Holy Spirit to draw you near to the Lord. Jesus has sent our comforter, the Holy Spirit to guide us. We will see God clearly if we listen to the prompting to spend time in His Word.

God's love is amazing. Maybe early one morning you will be awaken by the Lord asking you, "What do you want from Me?" We limit God's love, He doesn't. Allow Him the opportunity to show you His love. He wants to show His love and take your burdens and give you rest. Only you can let go and give Him your burdens and accept His gift of love.

Come unto me, all ye that labour and are heavy laden, and I will give you rest. Take my yoke upon you, and learn of me: for I am meek and lowly in heart; and ye shall find rest unto your souls. For my yoke is easy and my burden is light. (Matthew 11:28-30)

This yoke the scripture is speaking of is not another bondage you will be placed under. This yoke is as a friend with his arm around your shoulders. Where you walk He will walk with you. When you struggle to get up the mountains and when you walk down through the valleys, He will help you with the load. Like horses which are placed together in tandem to pull a wagon or a heavy load, your pace will go step-in-step with the Lord if you will let Him. Like the tandem horses, if one gets upset the other is able to settle him down. Doesn't that sound great? You can know you will never have to walk alone. God will comfort you so you don't have to struggle and His love will carry you through.

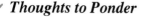

Thoughts to Ponder

Have you ever felt burdened down by life's problems?

Do you ever wonder how you will ever make it on your own?

Jesus has offered to help us with any burden we are called to carry.

> *Come unto me, all ye that labour and are heavy laden, and I will give you rest. Take my yoke upon you, and learn of me: for I am meek and lowly in heart; and ye shall find rest unto your souls. For my yoke is easy and my burden is light.* (Matthew 11:28-30)

Why don't you sit down and spend time with Him right now and ask Him for His help. God loved you so much He sent His only Son to die for you on the cross at Calvary. Why would you refuse such a wonderful gift? Reach out and accept it today. Then share all of your burdens with your new best friend, Jesus Christ. He stands at the door waiting for you to invite Him into your life.

> *Behold, I stand at the door, and knock: if any man hear my voice, and open the door, I will come in to him, and will sup with him, and he with me.* (Revelation 3:20)

Why not thank your heavenly Father right now for the gift of His Son, Jesus Christ? Then share your burdens with Him and tell Him you need His help each and every day. He is just waiting for your call!

Chapter 21

TIME FLIES BY

Ever wonder how time has gotten away from you? I know I certainly have, and time seems to fly faster the older I get. It makes me wonder how in the world did I get this old this fast.

When I was young my Grandmother would tell me about how time flew away from her and she said the same would for me when I got older. I didn't see the concept of her thought, how could this be? There are only so many days in a year and so many hours in a day, minutes, and seconds and so on.

Now at my age I can see that Grandma was right on. The minutes seem to elude me and one more day is gone. I still need more time to accomplish my "to do" list in any one day. It seems to have flown by and I now have grown children and a great-granddaughter with one more on the way! Wow! When did I start this entire ball rolling? Of course, I do know when, but it seems an eternity ago and another world away. So much has changed in my life over the years.

I think of the small amount of time it took to get to my age. In that amount of time again I won't be on this earthly plane, I will be with the Lord.

So the question comes to mind what have I accomplished? Have my words helped others? Did I make a difference in this world? Will anyone remember any wisdom which I have passed on down through the generations? The questions go on as I search for the answers.

"What ifs" are far from us and we can only look forward in our walk of life. Things in the future are the things we can change. The past is gone forever and we can't change any of it. We can only hope we have learned and grown from the experiences this world has offered.

We were counting the amount of days I have lived and I could see others in the room were having the same questions and revelations in their minds. The questions came from them, what would others say at their funeral or celebration of life? The questions were asked from each of us and the answers of course became funny responses due to the great sense of humor of my friends and associates.

Make the Time Count

That morning when I was going into work I had seen a fabulous sunrise on my trip to town. I live a bit up over the town so it is awesome to see the mountain range in the mornings and evenings. I expressed to my friends and associates that we should make every wonderful sight count as we see it, and then I shared my experience of God's hand painting such an awesome sunrise scene. I was hoping others would take time out of their busy schedule to take a peek of its splendor as I sought to try to describe God's handiwork.

We'd had a few days of rain and the moisture from the dew was rising on the distant mountain some thirty miles away. A dusty blue rising from the earth, and a middle layer of another shade of lighter blue about a third of the way up the face of the mountainside mesmerized me. The palm trees dancing in the wind between me and the mountain range made them look as though they could walk away. The sun was creeping up the back side of the horizon placing a haunting echo of blue tones I had never seen before and would be surprised if I ever had that experience again. I have never seen another to compare to the shades painted by God's hand that morning inspiring me to share with you.

I know God paints us some of the most beautiful sunrises and sunsets in Arizona; some of the prettiest of any state I have lived in. Our thunderstorms electrify the sky line with bolts of intense lightning. At times I have seen lightning strike palm trees and the fruit explode into glaring fire balls flying from the tree as if they were fireworks from the Fourth of July.

One day I was out horseback riding with friends and saw a rainbow, God's covenant arch of promise as it raced across the skies and landed on a saguaro cactus. What a sight to see! It was so amazing that even the horses were looking at it. This made us recall the gold at the end of the rainbow we had heard of from fairytales, but we already had the gold from the experience of witnessing something so miraculous. This memory is one of those moments in my life I won't forget.

God is such an awesome God to give us all these wonderful rays of colors making our minds dance with delight! I am thrilled to have the ability to see and smell the jasmine and roses, the smell of leather when walking into a barn where the horses have been working and their tack is all cleaned up after a good ride. It places a picture in my mind from the smell of some of my favorite times in the past with my horses.

There is nothing like the touch of a friend to lets you know how much they care. A smile from a stranger reminding you we all live in a great big living room where someone is willing to stand up and let us sit down. The glance from your spouse across the room, knowing they are thinking of you romantically as the chatter and clatter of the room roars around them. Feeling the eyes of a dear friend in need, hoping you will notice without a word being expressed. Then there is the taste of a hot cup of coffee in the morning as you watch while the morning arises and allow the aroma of the morning tease your senses or a glass of wine to celebrate after you have survived another hectic day.

Of course there is the joy of picking up our children, holding them close, and never growing so old that we can't tell our children how much we love them. Having grandchildren and seeing the love in our children's eyes for their children insures the love will continue through the generations. When we are able to see how much we love our children, we know God loves us even better than we could even imagine. How exciting it is!

Each day our lives are touched by miracles and amazing beauty which have been supplied for us from the hand of God! It is time to slow down and smell the roses as they say; this world was created for each and every one of us to enjoy. What a wonderful God and Master we serve when we learn to lean on Him and enjoy this awesome ride He has prepared for each of us, including you. Time does seem to fly and it is our choice to reach out and walk with our Lord while enjoying this time we have with Him.

Take time to give that smile to a stranger, it can make all the difference in the world. I once walked by a gentle giant of a man that looked as if he couldn't walk another day. I smiled and told him, "Smile, God loves you'" and walked on. Later he became brave enough to come into the salon where I was working and asked me if I remembered him, and of course I did. He was the gentle giant who looked like he needed to know someone cared.

He told me he was praying that morning and told God it felt like no one, not even God, cared for him. He had been asking himself why he should live another day. He said he was going to the bank to get his affairs in order when I happened to be coming out of the bank and told him, "Smile, God loves you." I knew he had looked a bit surprised by the statement, but I felt the urge to tell him, so I did. He expressed his appreciation and I reminded him it was true and threw him another smile. A smile came across his face and I knew he had been touch by the hand of God through the Holy Spirit.

When you see something exceptional remember God has inspired it. When you feel you should smile and say, "Hi" or "God loves you," regardless of what society says, run with it! You will be amazed at God's grace and mercy! You may make a difference in someone else's life. Our time flies by so quickly, we need to make it count! God will give you many opportunities to enjoy the workmanship of His hand if you take the time to look for it. Enjoy it because this is the day the Lord has made. We need to rejoice and be glad in it. God made it all for you and for me!

This is the day the LORD has made; We will rejoice and be glad in it. (Psalm 118:24)

Thoughts to Ponder

Do you realize the wondrous beauty God has placed all around you?

When was the last time you really enjoyed a beautiful sunrise or sunset?

Can you enjoy the amazing power released in a lightning storm?

Don't let time run away without enjoying all that the Lord has put in place for you. Take the time to enjoy your family and friends each and every day. Stop and smell the roses along the way and thank your Heavenly Father who has given you such a beautiful world to live and thrive in.

Pray: *Thank You, Father God for this beautiful world You have given me. Thank You for my dear family and friends. This is the day You have made especially for me and I will rejoice and be glad in it.*

Chapter 22

ARE YOU TOO BUSY?

This is a question that many would answer yes to, but how do they stop being busy and become productive in their life? Most people will ask you off handedly, "What have you been up to?" The usually the reply is, "Oh, I've been so busy! Not sure what I've been up to, but I sure have been busy."

One has to ask themselves how in the world has this happened. Who makes me so busy I don't get anything done? Why am I so exhausted at the end of the day and still wonder what I have accomplished? What warrants spending a whole day doing, but at the end of the day I am not sure what it was I was so busy doing? Over and over the questions become even more confusing when one is trying to figure it out.

Recently I was in Branson, Missouri and let me tell you, one can be very busy there and never accomplish all the things you had in mind. My husband asked me as we traveled down the main strip if I saw this show's advertisement and then another and on and on. Soon my brain felt like I was on overload. I told him I needed to focus on what we intended to do while we were there, and try to ignore all those other flashing lights that were trying to pull us off focus.

I feel life is like that. When you want to relax and have some down time, it seems everywhere you turn there is something flashing trying to get your attention. In Phoenix where I live they have signs now that change so quickly you are not sure you saw what you thought you were looking at seconds earlier. I think being bombarded by all of this is not a good thing and could easily distract us from what and where we are supposed to be.

When God told us in the Bible to be aware of what our eyes see and what our ears hear, I think it is very relevant to the times we live in. So many parents fall into the pattern of running their children from one event to another complaining they are too busy, but they are the ones that set the agenda in place. What are we thinking when we start these balls rolling. Does all this running from event to event teach our children to effectively use the gifts God has given them while here on earth? We have not taught our children the benefits of down time to see and hear what their gifts are and how God would have them use them for His kingdom purposes.

God will reveal these things to us if we will be still and not have the chatter of radio, TV, and all the other gadgets playing constantly. I hear that most men do not like to be without sound. Is it because we don't want to hear what God is trying to tell us? I know some women say they want to hear from God and want to know how to do it. But are they willing to take the time to find out, spend time in the Word, and learn to hear the Lord's voice clearly? Or do we all say we are just too busy?

How do we stop this vicious cycle of busyness and begin to gain control of our lives? If we don't figure it out, how are we going to teach our children how to do it? We have to set boundaries for ourselves and protect our children by doing the same for them and teach them to live within those boundaries. Let's teach them to hear from the Lord when they are young, and then their lives will be much more meaningful without all the busyness. When the trials come, and we all know they will come, they will know how to stand still where they are until they hear from the Holy Spirit.

When we don't know what to do, we could take off on a path we shouldn't be on and lose all concept of common sense. When we take off running in every direction and none in particular, we are a bit out of control. We can't hear from God when we are frantic. God has given us a sound mind as it says in 2 Timothy 1:7. Let's remember if we have a sound mind then we have to stop long enough to listen to and use what it is telling us instead of running off haphazardly until we run into a brick wall.

Have you ever watched a horse run away when it gets scared? The quarter horse is called a quarter horses because of the fright and flight reflexes God has given them to protect themselves. The horse will run a quarter mile and then finally stop and turn to see what scared them. That is how we will react if we aren't grounded in the word so we can know where we stand. Greater is He that is in me than he that is in the world (see 1 John 4:4). Let's be aware of what we allow Satan to make us fearful of and remember fear is really False Evidence Appearing Real.

I have a list in place where I think of the three most important things I should spend time doing every day, then another three for the week, the month, the next six months, and the year. If you take the time to sit alone in the quiet and ask God to help you with your list, I think you will find your life will become less busy and more orderly. I will go into this more in the next chapter, but I can assure you God is not about confusion. He is all about keeping things in their proper order. I know we all have things we need to get done, but by choosing wisely we can actually accomplish more in the same period of time. Look how far you have come in age in your life at this time. When we think how fast life has come and will soon be gone, it is important not to throw our time away. We need to make it count.

Make time with God one of the three things you choose to spend your time on daily because He can make the rest of the time in your life go much farther. He is the designer of person, place, things, and time. He will help you seriously think about what is really important in your life. You were made precious in His eyes, and He wants the best for you. Remember He is your Heavenly Father.

When my husband and I decided to take the trip to Branson, we needed to get away from all the distractions in our everyday life and spend some quality time together. We were meeting some friends there and looking forward to our time with them also, yet we were determined to take some time for us alone as well. If we were not careful, all the bright lights and signs could have distracted us from receiving God's best for us on our little vacation.

At home we have a regiment that takes us from work, to dinner, do a few chores and that is all she wrote, as they say. I have to do laundry, dishes, and straighten up the house, but busyness does not have to rob me of my peace and joy. So where do we start putting our boundaries down and enforcing them? I will offer some practical suggestions in the next chapter, but for now take a few minutes to stop and think about what God is saying to you for today.

Be still, and know that I am God: I will be exalted among the heathen, I will be exalted in the earth. (Psalm 46:10)

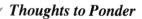

Thoughts to Ponder

Do you realize you were made precious in God's eyes?

Do you understand He wants the best for you every day?

Won't you take the time to sit still and get to know Him?

Pray: *Father God, remind me to take the time to stop and sit with You each and every day so that I can know You and receive Your plan for my day. Thank You that You only want the very best for Me.*

Chapter 23

BOUNDARIES

I t has come to my attention that not enough is taught about how to stabilize our boundaries. I hear people talking about enabling and not really helping others; not knowing how to place the boundaries in place and how to stand and not be moved. I have people ask me all the time to be on this committee or to join another organization and help with them. I have to say, "No, I am sure you will find someone more suitable for the job." It is only two letters, "no," and I have to make myself stay within my boundaries understanding that my energy and time cannot be stretched where I am not effective. Giving them a little "sugar," by encouraging them to find someone else more suitable, helps the "medicine" of your refusal go down easier so they might not be as offended.

Not everyone is going to be happy when we place our boundaries. We need to pray about what boundaries God wants us to put in place. I'm asked often just how you do that. I think first we have to find a balance and then we can more effectively set in the place the proper boundaries to achieve and keep that balance in our lives.

You need to take this planning process seriously. It is not a quick thought to be thrown into a bag to mill around. You need to honestly ponder what you put on these lists. It may take you a day or two to think of what to put on these lists and how to answers these questions. You also need to realize the dedication and investment you will need to truly achieve balance, order, and peace in your life. If that is your desire, let's begin the process.

First: List the three most important things you spend your time doing daily—such as time with your spouse, your children, with God, music, animals, job, etc.

Second: What are the three most important things you wish to accomplish this next week other than the daily things that are on List 1? This will be List 2. Examples might be: Organize your closet, finish a project you have started, clean the car, or straighten up your home. How can God trust us with things from His heavenly Home when we won't keep ours in order?

Third: What do you want to accomplish in the next month? Perhaps clean up your file cabinet or sort out your closet and send some of your clothes to those in need. This is List 3.

Now post these lists where you can see them and be reminded of them every day. Now it is time to be a doer and begin doing what you have listed. When we look at these lists it can seem overwhelming at first, but God will give us the ability to go through the tasks He gives us. He will never send us where He cannot be there to help when we do our part. He does expect us to finish things He sets us to task to accomplish.

I think by listing your daily tasks it begins to help you to set your major boundaries. Come hell or high water, these are things that you need to set your mind to, be dedicated to, and make sure you have the time to accomplish. If you have a spouse, there are specific things God has instructed for you to do within your marriage. Am I saying marriage is work? Marriage is probably the toughest job you will ever do. Placing someone else's feeling in front of yours, and going the extra mile to meet their needs makes marriage a worthwhile endeavor, but it is work nonetheless. The benefits you reap include knowing your spouse is there with you and has your back no matter what comes at the two of you in the future.

If you have children, a portion of time needs to be spent on them, but once again, God tells us that your spouse comes first and the children are to grow up and leave to find their own spouses.

With Lists #2 and #3, when you have accomplished the tasks on your list, DO NOT ADD MORE THINGS until you reach the end of the designated time frame! If you see the list every day, you will probably have it done before the end of the week. We are not like children in school and there is not a punishment for having your work done at the very last minute because you procrastinated. However, implementing this plan gives you a tool to help you not only accomplish what needs to be done, but help you learn to stay within your boundaries and not be overwhelmed. The extra time you will discover you have when your life is balanced and orderly is a reward.

At the end of the first week and your list is all done, then you start a new list for the next week, to be accomplished before that week is done. Once again, when your list is done, do not find many more things to do and wear yourself out to where your family is not enjoying your company. You will find accomplishing your designated tasks gives you permission to do some of the enjoyable things that you never seem to have time to do when your time is not focused on what you have determined is important. It is very freeing and rewarding experience.

Please take the time when you make your lists. This is something that warrants your dedication if you not only want to accomplish your goals but be effective in using your gifts and talents the way God has designed you. For example, making cookies can be one of those tasks that will reap dual benefits. Get your family involved even if it seems more of a hassle. While they are making cookies with you, they will start talking to you and you can learn an unending amount of information about what is going on with their lives. These are things they need to tell you, but Satan keeps us so busy with distractions like those flashing, blinking lights in Branson that we are changing directions every so many seconds. It's amazing how we can get distracted from what is really important in our lives by what the world is screaming at us. Choose the things on your list carefully and learn to set your boundaries wisely and you will reap amazing benefits.

When you have started on your program of organizing your life, completing every task will become easier. If you have a list when you go to the grocery store and only stick to that, you will be in and out of the store more quickly, saving money and time. The rest of the things that try to get your attention while walking through the store are just distractions; things you would probably not really use and would waste your money and time. Ever get home, unpack your grocery bags and wonder why in the world you bought that? Want to stop wondering why you did the things you did during the day and why you didn't accomplish anything meaningful? Invest in organizing your life and begin to accomplish more while feeling frustrated less.

He is not a God of confusion and disorder but of peace and order. (1 Corinthians 14:33 AMP)

Thoughts to Ponder

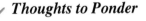

As you start making your lists and organizing your life, you will find that each time you stay the course, you will reap amazing benefits. It may take you a little extra time to carefully consider what is important in your life and what your true priorities are, but the end benefit will far outweigh the extra time you invest.

Don't wait another day to begin to eliminate confusion and begin to bring order into your life. Ask God to help direct your paths and He will bring you not only productivity but peace.

Pray: *Thank You, Father God that You are a God of peace and order. Help me to diligently begin to follow Your path by bringing order to my life. Help me to take each day as a gift and determine to accomplish what You say is important. Help me to ignore the distractions and focus on You.*

Chapter 24

THE COVENANT OF MARRIAGE

O ne of the places that can be adversely affected by our busy hectic lifestyles is marriage. Not only is busyness an issue, at this time in our country there seems to be a major struggle going on about marriage and family values. The answers to this dilemma are found in our inspiring living Word of God, the Bible. This is the only place we can start and finish our thoughts when we search for the answers to any of our questions about life. This marvelous Book holds all the answers and has stood the test of time.

The problem we run into is when myth or opinion begins to overshadow Truth. A myth or opinion is true some of the time, for some of the people, and in some situations. Truth is rooted in God's Word which is true for all people, all the time, and in all situations.[1]

The Bible states in Genesis 1:27-28 that God made male and female and blessed them. God told them to be fruitful, multiply, replenish the earth, and subdue it. They were to have dominion over every living thing that moved on the earth.

---

1   Dr. Larry Keefauver from his book, *The 77 Irrefutable Truths of Marriage*

The woman was created to help man because God saw it was not good for man to be alone. The very fact that woman was made from man's rib is an amazing truth from God's Word.

And the rib, which the Lord God had taken from man, make He a Woman, and brought her unto the Man.

And Adam said, This is now bone of my bones, and flesh of my flesh; she shall be called Woman, because she was taken out of Man.

Therefore shall a man leave his father and his mother and shall cleave unto his wife; and they shall be one flesh. (Genesis 2:22-24)

Hence we have marriage where a ring is given to symbolize the full circle of love between God, man, woman, and the creation process. When we make this covenant between husband and wife in marriage, it is one that is not to be taken lightly. There are reasons people get divorced and for many it is due to the safety of couples and their children. In my book, *On Fire for God*, I explain a situation like this due to dangerous conditions in our home. No one is victorious in these circumstances of divorce and you feel as if a piece of you has been torn from you which cannot be corrected or mended.

However, in most cases, when times are hard we need to go back and remember the reason we love our spouses and why God placed them in our lives. We all want to think these times will not come to us, but they do because we are all human and we all have failings. I know I have my share, and my husband is a saint to look passed them and love me despite my faults.

A spouse should be our best friend. I know there has to be that spark between you both, but it will not last if that is what you base your marriage relationship on. Your spouse should be able to love you unconditionally and vice versa, which is almost impossible except through the Lord's love. You do this by placing God first in your marriage.

God sees us as one when we make this covenant through marriage. Speaking lovingly to one another is one thing that takes considerable effort at times because of the issues God is working within us. Words cannot be placed back in your mouth and eaten after they have been spilled out. Once hurtful words are spoken they are out there and they cut to the soul. Please think carefully before you say harsh words to your other half. Forgiveness can be given, but words cannot be taken back.

Sometimes just a short walk to the other room to ask God to guide you will help. Many times I have learned to be silent; the old saying, "Silence is golden" is certainly true. In my case I have much more of an issue with it than my husband. He will just give me a look of, "Are you okay?" Then I will stop and reflect on what I am saying and doing at the time. He gives me much space to deal with these issues which apparently I need at times.

A few years ago as I did my daily reading from the Bible, it seemed the words, "be silent" echoed in my spirit for nearly a week. Then I read that it was better to live on the roof top than to live with a nagging wife. Ouch! Over and over again for a whole week the scriptures kept taking me back to the phrase "be silent." If you only knew me you would know that is one of the hardest things for me to do. For some reason I seem to have much to say, if you know what I mean. I found that week to be a growing experience and a tough one at that (Proverbs 21:9; Proverbs 25:24).

That particular week my husband was trying to make some decisions and he was not able to gain a peace about them. He was having a tough time working them through. When we are in struggle mode God will not help until we stop and ask for help from Him. Then He will be glad to help as any good parent would do.

As the week wore on I became very quiet. God, of course, was right. I needed to be silent and let God work with my husband. It is incredible what He can do if we are silent and let Him do the fixing. We are not to be the fixers of our spouses. We married our spouses and loved them the way they were then; God will heal the other things with us and our partners that are surfacing now.

Being married has been one of the hardest jobs I have ever done. I was divorced sixteen years and raised my children by myself. What I decided would always be the deciding factor. I tried to make the best decisions I could for my little family though I stumbled and fell many times. When I married again and we become one it was no longer about me and my wants and my wishes. Now it was about what was best for the both of us together.

Our spouses have to be placed first in our minds and hearts. This is true love when we can accept our spouses, see their flaws as their attributes, and learn from them. Many times the things that bug us the most are the things we don't like about ourselves. I know it is hard to take a good look at the reflection in the mirror at times.

There is nothing like enjoying our children sent to us from God. What a miracle it is to be given a child for us to mentor from our Heavenly Father. I think life would be much easier if we could keep in our minds that they aren't really our children, but our Father's children.

God should always be first, our spouse second, and then our children. Children are the fruit of our love and they are to grow up and become productive adults. Many will get married and become one with their spouse and possibly have fruit in their relationships that are children sent from God. I also think it is very important our children realize we are human. Placing us on a pedestal only gives us the opportunity to fall, and fall we will, being human. Thank goodness for God's grace and our children's ability to forgive us when we fall.

In the Bible we are given a scriptural description of the virtuous woman. Proverbs 31:10-31 is a lot to live up to, but also gives us something to strive towards in God's eyes. I challenge you to take time and go through these scriptures and find all the wonderful things you already accomplish.

Married life can be a delightful experience and one of the most fulfilling ones you can have. If you are married, take time to thank God for the spouse He has picked for you. If you are not married, pray about a spouse that God would want for you. Make your list of what you hope for in a spouse and be specific, God likes that. We have not because we ask not (James 4:2).

Thoughts to Ponder

Do you realize your spouse is a gift from God? Do you take the time to thank God for this precious gift?

Do you tell your spouse what a precious gift from God they are to you?

Think about the way you felt about each other before you were married. Review the marriage vows you spoke one to another on that day. Now remember that you spoke those vows before God and that He expects you to keep them.

Married life can be a delightful experience and one of the most fulfilling relationships you can have. It is hard work, but God is there to help and guide you every step of the way if you will make Him the third strand in your marriage bond.

Read Ecclesiastes 4:9-12.

Two are better than one, because they have a good reward for their labor. For if they fall, one will lift up his companion. But woe to him who is alone when he falls, for he has no one to help him up. Again, if two

*lie down together, they will keep warm; But how can
one be warm alone? Though one may be overpowered
by another, two can withstand him. And a threefold
cord is not quickly broken.* (NKJV)

Thank God right now for the spouse He has given you or
the spouse He is going to give you. Remind yourself everyday
what a wonderful gift God has given you in your spouse.

Chapter 25

THE BLESSINGS OF A MOM

A mother is the one you should be able to go to when you have a hurt, a scrape on your knee or elbow as a child. As young adults, our mothers should give us comfort as we grow through the struggles in our lives. They are to be mentors for us as the biblical description of a godly wife and mother says in Proverbs 31:10-31. She gets up every morning and starts the day before the rest of the household does, caring for her husband and family. This is what I feel a mother should be, but sadly that is not reality in our society at this present time.

I missed out on a mother that loved that way. Now that I am grown and have children of my own, I would like to think my husband and I love our children unconditionally as the Bible instructs. We might not always like the way our children are acting; maybe not finding them very pleasant as they grow and rebel, however, the fact remains we still love our children regardless.

In my book, "On Fire for God," I describe my life as a child. I will briefly recap what life was like for me and my siblings growing up with a mother who suffered a grand mall seizure while we were still young that left her with what would be called multiple personalities and diagnosed as bipolar by today's standard. Our lives were in danger daily and we never knew what might set mother off into one of these episodes. She would snap and you would hope you were not where you could be reached. The saying walk lightly as if walking on eggs certainly applied at our home.

Many nights we would find her wondering around with a knife heading into someone's bedroom. We all slept very lightly and would be listening for steps in the night to protect one another. We were a very close knit family and cared for each other. I guess you could say we covered each others' backs as the saying goes. For us it was a matter of survival.

Sis got married and left home first and my older brother was next to go. I came along next and was married at fifteen. When my first child was born I was only sixteen at that time and had a husband that had been in an accident and had to have major care. All this seemed to be a bit much to bear at the tender age of sixteen.

Though my mother was not able to help me become a godly mother, my Grandmother had been a mentor for me all of her life. She would never give me the answer to a question, but would ask me a question that would lead me to find the answer for myself. She would have been a great psychologist!

Expressing to my Grandmother that I wasn't sure how to care for this new little bundle of joy that I loved so much, she told me all I had to do was feed and love him a lot and God would take care of the rest. She assured me if I did then he would grow up just fine. Time went by and it was as Grandmother had told me. I loved him a lot, fed him when he was hungry, and God took care of the rest. Grandmother was a wise woman and just as she had spoken to me, my son did grow up and became a successful adult and a wonderful father that cares deeply for his own family. I am deeply proud of him!

Growing up with a dysfunctional mother, I always wished I had one that was like my friends' parents. They were happy to see their children, morning, noon, and night. Maybe because I had not experienced such love for myself, when I was with my friends and they greeted their moms I noticed a twinkle would appear in their eyes. I didn't understand it then, but now that I am a mom I have to admit there is nothing like hearing your children calling you mom. I like to think my eyes twinkle when my children call me mom and want to talk with me about what is going on in their lives.

Imagine how God feels when we call Him, "Abba Father."

 ### *Thoughts to Ponder*

As you read about my childhood experiences with my mother, did you think about your experiences with your own mother? Are your thoughts of the good times or the bad times? Perhaps there are issues in your life that stem from not having resolved problems in your relationship with your mother. The Bible says we are to honor our fathers and our mothers because if we do it will affect our later lives (see Exodus 20:12). Ask Your Heavenly Father to reveal areas you may have to forgive your mother, and ask forgiveness from her. Also pray and ask the Father to forgive you for those times you did not honor your mother.

Pray: *Heavenly Father, thank You for Your uncondi-tional love for me. Help me to love my children with that same love. Please show me where I have not obeyed You in honoring my own mother. Please forgive me for those times and help me to forgive my mother for those times she wounded me. Help me to restore any breeches in my relationship with my mother.*

Chapter 26

GOD BRINGS ME A MOM

My children are all grown and I am proud to be called their mother. We have helped raise two nephews also and I love them as if they were our own children. God has brought me this godly man to be my husband whom I couldn't have picked on my own. He supports me in the ministry and whatever I put my hand to.

When we moved to the Casa Grande, Arizona area, I started working at a hair salon which had several stylists. One of the stylists had a mother-in-law that was a precious godly woman and if the stylist was out for a vacation I would do her mother-in-law's hair. I enjoyed her very much. She made porcelain dolls that were life-like and I would purchase them and send them to my Aunt HaHa who had a doll collection. My Aunt was a wonderful mentor in my life and helped care for my son when my daughter was in the hospital so many times when she was young.

Later, I opened my own salon and once again God answered my prayer in a very unusual way. This stylist ended up with a bad health problem and never returned to hairdressing. Her mother-in-law came and asked if I would do her hair full time to which I readily agreed! Everyone called her Mama B, and I asked if I might as well. She thought that would be just fine. When we discussed the price to do her hair, I told her I wished to use the money toward some dolls if that would seem fitting for her. We agreed and started a tally on how much for each of these wonderful dolls. She had one doll that sucked its thumb just like my daughter had when she was small so I picked that one for her. These dolls are the most life-like I have ever seen. I'd spend time at Mama B's to figure out which doll to bring home and will always cherished that time we spent together.

Mama B is this small delightful godly woman that anyone would be proud to call their mom. She has a complexion that is so porcelain that the times of heartache and trials show clearly on her face. However, when she smiles you can see the light of the Lord shining through and it warms my soul. She has this adorable pleasant sounding voice and still sings in her church choir. Family is the most valuable thing in her life other than the Lord and she has the gift of being an intercessory prayer warrior.

Within a year of getting to know her, I was spending many days thinking of her and on the spur of the moment I'd call and ask if she would like to go shopping with me or even take a break for lunch. If possible she would and we had many great times together. She is married to this godly man who just lights up when he sees her come into the room. There is no doubt in my mind he would do anything she asked within his grasp.

One day at the shop when she wanted to know how much she owed me, I told her that I had stopped keeping track of the amount nine months previously. Of course she wanted to argue with me about paying with the dolls, but I told her how much she meant to me and I'd no longer accept anything for doing her hair. I'd grown to love this godly woman who filled the empty spot in my heart for a mother. She comes to get her hair done every Friday and it brightens my day. I book out extra time for this wonderful woman I call "Mom."

Friends have told me God gives us children, yet I know I am loved by this blessed woman as her child. Most people in town think she is my mother and you know, I couldn't be more honored. She calls me her second daughter and I stand tall knowing she loves me, too. I praise the Lord for giving me the desires of my heart and for sending me a mother who tells me if she thinks I am making a bad decision, comes to the hospital when I'm ill, shows up at my events, and loves to go shopping and out for a meal with me. I can share anything with her and I know she loves me unconditionally! What more could I have asked for.

Several scriptures from the Psalms come to mind as I conclude this chapter.

Psalm 37:4 says, "Delight thyself also in the LORD: and he shall give thee the desires of thine heart."

Psalm 27:10 reads, "Even if my father and mother abandon me, the LORD will hold me close" (NLT).

Psalm 68:5 declares, "A father of the fatherless, a defender of widows, is God in His holy habitation" (NKJV).

Thoughts to Ponder

 What a wonderful loving Heavenly Father we have who cares for us as a loving parent. He loves to give us the desires of our hearts, and He cares for us and loves even when we are unlovely and rejected by everyone else in our world. Take time to thank Him every day for His great love, protection, and blessing in your life.

Pray: *Thank You Heavenly Father that You love me even when I am unlovely. Thank You that You never abandon or reject me though everyone else in my life might. Thank You that You desire to give me the desires of my heart. Help me to reflect Your love to others today knowing You have blessed me to be a blessing to others.*

Chapter 27

BROKEN PIECES

"Dysfunctional" is a term used to describe many families today, but where does that dysfunction start from? It actually began from the very first bit of time when Adam and Eve fell from grace in the garden and sin fell on them. They created the dysfunctional family. Their son Cain killed his brother Abel from simple jealousy. Their lives were broken and until the Potter, our Father in heaven paid the price with His Son, we were all destined to live dysfunctional lives.

We see broken pieces of our lives caused by tribulation like the fracturing of a ceramic vase when it is shaken or dropped. Only when we come to God, the potter, can He put our lives back together into something better than when we started. The original pattern has been broken by sin, but the re-molding will in the end be even more magnificent.

I have learned a lot from my adopted mom and her husband who make porcelain dolls from the slip; the liquid that is poured into a mold. Pouring the slip is the first step of the long process. It has to be poured very carefully or a bubble will be in the mold that if left undetected will ruin the final product.

One day MaMa B decided that I should help make my own doll so her husband got out the molds and I started with pouring the slip. What a mess I had all over myself. The slip even splashed up onto my face.

Dad laughed as he said, "All the dolls I've poured I've never gotten slip on my face."

I laughed as I realized I had the slip on my hands, arms, and my face. I told them I thought maybe that's what a mud bath feels like. Wow, what a mess!

Then the waiting process starts. You can't leave the house for more than an hour and a half because the slip cannot be left in the mold beyond that. Then you have to check to see if it comes loose from the mold easily. If it is ready, then oh so carefully so it won't cave in, you tenderly remove the slip from the mold which is now called green ware. This green ware is then place carefully on something very soft so it won't break while it sits for a few days. Reminds us of how fragile we are as babies doesn't it?

After it has set a few days it can be picked up carefully and the potter then removes all the seam marks left from the mold. Believe me this is not an easy task. I broke the finger off the first hand I tried to work on. I wanted so desperately to make my first doll myself.

When the finger broke off I wanted Mom to fix it, but she just smiled and said, "I knew you were going to do that, you were trying too hard to make it perfect. We will put it back with the old slip and after a couple days we will be able to pour a new doll with it."

That did make me feel a bit better that it was not totally wasted. This reminds us of how we try to be perfect, which is of course impossible. Many think they have to get themselves clean and free of any of these blemishes before they can come to the Potter for salvation. That is the farthest thing from the truth. He is our maker and He will be the one who is our finisher. We can come to Him broken; He can use the broken pieces and make something wonderful.

Once the green ware was dried, it was time to lightly bore out where the eyes were to be placed in the doll with a special tool. When Mom told me I was going to work on it, I wanted her to do that for me.

But as a true mentor she said, "No, this is your doll and I will help when you need it, but you haven't even tried."

She was right, I had not tried yet. God is like that, He wants us to try and He stands by because He knows we will need help. He has given us the tools to do the task and wants us to get started, but He is always there ready to help when we call. As a matter of fact He has promised He will never leave nor forsake us (see Joshua 1:5).

I guess you have figured it out by now. Yes, I ruined the head because I bored the eyes until they looked scary. No eyes could have fit into the giant eye holes I created. When I tried too hard to make it perfect again the piece was ruined. Mom just laughed and I wanted to cry. It was a scary looking thing, not at all the picture I had in my mind for my doll.

Have you figured out the connection God has revealed to me? Our lives are much like the times we try hard to make everything perfect. It is impossible without going back to our heavenly Father and asking for some grace and mercy to make it all right. Thank goodness that is always available much like Mom who didn't leave me. I would see her smiling as she worked next to me and we had a great time talking. The same is true of our Father in heaven who wants to visit and talk with us. What a great gift to realize we are that loved by Him, our Potter.

We worked on the doll for several days and it was still far from finished. After the green ware was filed where the seams no longer showed and the eyes were bored, it had to be placed in the kiln and cooked.

How many of us know what it is like to be cooked? Sometimes we want to be removed from the heat before God says that it's just right.

145

I'm sure I am not the only one that has stood at the window of the kiln as it's cooking me crying, "I don't think I can take any more."

Then we hear the comforting voice from the Potter saying, "Just a bit more. I am with you even in the fire."

I worked on the pieces that had been placed in the kiln. You have to wait again until they cool and sit for a couple days before you can work on the pieces again. The next step is to sand the pieces and make them smooth so they can be painted. You can see that your hard work is coming together, but you are still far from finished. Each piece is stronger at this point due to the cooking in the kiln and easier to work with. It will not break as easily. I liked that part and felt more confident as I sanded. Of course I enjoyed my precious time with Mom, visiting as we worked. She loves doing all the detail work and knowing she was right there with me gave me confidence to complete the process.

After sanding the dolls, the color is painted on them. Mom asked if I'd like to paint my little girl doll's face. By now I had already heard many stories about how a doll looked a mess because the painting was too much before placed back into the kiln.

My answer was, "No, Mom, please help me with that. I don't want to mess up after all this hard work."

I have to admit that Mom did most of the work, but she also allowed me to help and see all the work involved in making a doll. Because of this I appreciate the hard work put into each and every one. I did appreciate Mom's hard work and love for each doll she took special care to create. Do we know how much our Potter loves us and cares for each doll He has made?

Mom was awesome in finishing the doll for me. I know many more steps went into my little girl to make her the perfect little porcelain doll I cherish. She was right, all the work we put into her made the doll an extra special doll to me. This is the only one I worked on with my Mom.

Our lives bring us many tribulations and trials, but we must allow God to gather the broken pieces of our lives and remold us into what He wishes for us. He may need to crush a few pieces down into dust so we can be placed back on the potter's wheel and remade. We cannot continue when we are broken and overwhelmed. We need to go to the Lord and He will work us into something magnificent for Him.

But now, O LORD, You are our Father; we are the clay, and You our potter; and we all are the work of Your hand. (Isaiah 64:8 NKJV)

Thoughts to Ponder

God is our maker and He will be the one who is our finisher. We can come to Him broken. He can use the broken pieces and make something wonderful. We cannot continue when we are broken and overwhelmed. We need to go to the Lord and He will work us into something magnificent for Him. We must be patient and trust that the Potter will do what is best for us, even when we have to go through the fire. He has promised He will never leave us nor forsake us (Joshua 1:5).

Pray: *Thank You, God that You are my Father and I am the clay. You are my potter and the work of Your hand. Thank You that even when You need to put me through the fire You have promised to never leave me alone. Thank You that I am never without You no matter what the circumstances all around me may look like. I trust You, Father God to take my broken pieces and make them into Your beautiful vessel.*

Chapter 28

WHAT PIECE ARE YOU?

When we would go and visit my grandmother's house there would always be an intricate puzzle displayed in the living room. We are much like the elaborate puzzles displayed in grandmother's home; it takes all the pieces to fall into place to make this beautiful picture.

Grandmother had some incredible puzzles that would sometimes take weeks to put together. My grandmother's mind was as quick later in life as it was early in her life. I often wondered if that was because her mind stayed so active.

These vivid colors from the puzzle pieces gave us many thoughts as to how they fit. Sometimes when you were sure you had the right fit, it would have a corner that no matter how you tried, it could not be squeezed into the point you thought was the perfect place. Are you an avid puzzle player? If you were part of the puzzle what piece would you like to be?

Many people come across my path and they are captive audiences when they come and sit in my chair. I am a hairdresser and they can't get up and run away, so the conversations we have are of many different colors, as they say. I hear many sad stories and many funny and inspiring ones. Of course I am a beautician not a magician, but I do pray for my clientele and hope they are able to glean something from their time with me. I feel everyone who comes and sits in my chair has been sent there, not by mishap but by God. Many times I am the one who receives the blessings from God by their time with me, which is always wonderful.

Sometimes we seem to think the place where we are is not the right fit for us. Perhaps that is because we do not see the big plan. We are as a piece of the puzzle and we can only see the pieces that are touching us or our piece that doesn't seem to fit anywhere.

When I started writing, I had no idea what God had planned for this book. I would sit down and write what the Lord had given me that day and continue the next time the same way. When I had about nineteen chapters finished, still not knowing what in the world they were all about, I decided to call Pamela, my editor. She is always a breath of fresh air from God with a heart that is led by the Holy Spirit and I trust her judgment.

I told her I had no idea what all this was about, but I had felt led to call her. Pamela told me to send it all her way and let her take a look. She promptly got back to me and was excited to see how all the chapters fell together for her. Now I couldn't see that until she pointed it out and put the pieces together. Pamela is another part of the intricate puzzle which makes all this work. Don't you agree we are blessed at what she does in the puzzle?

It is impossible to see what God has for the big picture unless we are willing to study His Word and see that His plan is much better than ours. It is not always easy to accept until we remind ourselves He is our heavenly Father. If we are parents we want what is good for our children. As children we know our parents want good for us, so how much more would our Heavenly Father give to us?

If ye then, being evil, know how to give good gifts unto your children, how much more shall your Father

*which is I heaven give good things to them that ask
him?* (Matthew 7:11)

We can struggle while we are in His hand as He places
us in our designated area in the puzzle, but the fact remains
we were designed for this purpose to fit in this spot where we
only see the pieces closest to us. Some are to be used as the
eye, the finger, the toe, the ear, the nose, and so on as we are
part of the body of Christ.

*Behold , I have graven thee upon the palms of
my hands, thy walls are continually before me.*
(Isaiah 49:16)

When I was young and my brothers got to go outside and
play, I always had to stay in the house and help clean, cook,
and sew. That was not what I wanted to do. I was constantly
telling my Grandmother, who was raising us at the time that
I wanted to be a boy. I didn't want to be a girl and have to be
inside while the boys were outside playing. It just didn't seem
fair to me. Why didn't they have to help with all the mess they
made on the floors when they came in from outside? Why did
the girls have to do it all?

I know every day I would make these statements about
how much I did not like being a girl; I wanted to go outside
and play! When I grew up I was going to get those paper
plates like those rich people had, was what I told everyone,
then I wouldn't have to do all those dishes. The girls were
the dish washers; we did not have an automatic dishwasher
at that time like we do now. I did enjoy being with my sister
and my grandmother, but still I couldn't take my eyes off of
how much fun the boys were having outside.

Finally, one day my grandmother told me to come and
sit with her for a bit. She had something to talk to me about.
Grandmother was a saint. Here she was taking care of four

children they'd been able to get custody of after almost two years in foster homes, and caring for her daughter who was learning to pick up buttons as a rehab from her grand mall seizure which had left her in a coma for over a year.

I was seven years old and I was not thinking about how Grandma was struggling to care for this readymade family of five. I was only seeing what I desired. She carefully sat me down and told me that she knew I might not understand this right now, but later in life I would come to understand what she was talking about. Grandmother said it was not always great to be one of the guys and that I should be happy that God made me who I was. He had not made a mistake making a young lady and there was a reason God had made me just as I was. She said one of these days I would see there are many things that women can do that men cannot do. When I was grown, married, and had a family I would understand why I was made as a woman.

She had a way of being convincing and I truly believed she was right. I decided to look forward to that time when I could understand. Of course the time came when I did understand; at that moment I remembered Grandma's words in my memory from years past. What a woman of God she was to take in this family and get them back to functional again which was another piece of the puzzle. More of that story can be read in my book, "On Fire for God."

The point, however, was I didn't want to be that piece in the puzzle that only got to do that one task. I wanted to be the other pieces, like the boys that seemed to have it better than I did. Don't miss being the awesome person God made you to be; YOU! You were created for this season and for a specific reason. You were created in this time to make a difference right where you are! God does not make junk. Search the Word and find out who you are in Christ. It will make you understand. We are the King's children and He wants us to be happy with what He made us to be.

And God said, Let us make man in our image, after our likeness: and let them have dominion over the fish of the sea and over the foul of the air, and over the cattle, and over all the earth, and over every creeping thing that creepeth upon the earth. So God created man in His own image, in the image of God created he him: male and female created he them. (Genesis 1:26-27)

For I know the plans I have for you, declared the Lord, plans to prosper you and not to harm you, plans to give you hope and a future. (Jeremiah 29:11 NIV)

Thoughts to Ponder

Did you, like the author, ever wish you were someone else growing up?

Did you ever feel like others got to do things you wished you could do?

Did you ever feel like God made a mistake in the way He made you?

Maybe you even felt He put you in the wrong family or the wrong time period. But did He?

Have you ever stood close to a painting and found you were unable to understand what the artist was trying to display?

What happened when you stood back away from it and could see the whole picture come together as the artist had designed it?

A puzzle is like that, too. When we look at all the separate pieces, we often cannot see the beautiful picture the fully assembled puzzle will create. Our lives are like that puzzle. God has placed us in His intricately designed puzzle. When we willingly submit to the way we were made, the place we are planted, and the position we are to fulfill, God's purpose is achieved. God's purpose always reveals a greater beauty than we could have ever imagined.

For my thoughts are not your thoughts, neither are your ways my ways, saith the LORD. (Isaiah 55:8)

Pray: *Thank You, Heavenly Father that as Your child, I can be secure in Your great plan for me. I desire to be all that You want me to be. I realize You have designed me for Your specific purpose and I want to fulfill that purpose. Help me to be patient, Lord, as I submit to and wait for Your plan to bring me to the place You want me to be.*

Chapter 29

AIRLINES AND ANGELS

Knowing that angels are protecting me and my family gives me faith to walk through life acknowledging God still cares. Life takes us to places we think we will never go. I had moved from state to state, not exactly sure I was where God wanted at that time. Finally my travels took me to Arizona to a town called Arizona City. I felt God had me where I was to be at that time in my life.

Arizona City was a quaint little town although its insight for growth was a bit before its time. It had a grocery store, a small library, a post office, and a cute little restaurant in this small gas station on the corner. It had great hamburgers and the cook/waitress made everyone feel welcome.

You could walk down the street and the thing that doesn't cost anything, a smile, would also bring a smile to the face of those you met. The people were cordial and it seemed everyone came from another part of the country and had come in search of a change in life. It was after I had moved to Arizona that my sister and I started singing together again although she lived about an hour and a half away. This made us set a time to practice our music. We deemed Wednesdays were the best. I would travel over first thing in the morning, we'd spend a couple hours practicing, she would feed me something, and I'd head back to work.

Our mother had moved from Illinois to Texas to be near one of my brothers who had children at home. Her wish was to spend some time with them. There were no children left in Illinois; we were scattered throughout the country. Mother had a severe stroke a few years before and had not recovered. She was diabetic now, had to take dialysis several times a week, and needed constant care. My brother had found this wonderful care facility for her to stay at that was not far from his home. This allowed him and the boys to come and visit easily.

Mother had been in Killeen for a couple months when I received a call from her doctor telling me Mother was in the hospital and he was not sure she was going to make it. He felt she was very unstable, and I should come quickly. I was at work when I received the call. Immediately I began praying for angels to clear the way for me to arrive safely and swiftly. A friend told me she would cancel my appointments for the next couple days and keep them abreast of the events.

Amazingly, a client worked in a travel agency that was a few doors down from the salon. I called and told this dear young friend of mine of the situation and that I needed to get there today. She promised she would do the best she could and would call as soon as she could arrange flight.

I called my husband and informed him of the doctor's request. He told me to be safe and let him know what was going on, and asked when was I going to be home? I said I really didn't know, but I felt the Lord was telling me to go as quickly as possible. I also called my sister and told her of the situation. She felt she needed to go and asked me to pick her up on the way to the airport. We prayed together before we hung up so she could get a ticket from her agency.

About that time I received a call from my friend at the travel agency and she had found me a flight for around three hundred dollars which was an unbelievable price for a same day flight. I told her she was a blessing and what a miracle that price was; she agreed. Sis called and said her flight was going to be over eight hundred.

I told her, "Let's pray about it again; maybe satan does not want us to go. We should raise our faith and speak angels to go out on our behalf to get better flight arrangements."

I told her to call the agency back and see if anything had changed. She quickly returned my call with a cheaper flight than mine. We both praised the Lord for sending His angels and making a way! The only thing which created an issue was we were traveling at different times. I had already made arrangements for a hotel and the car rental. My flight was about two hours before her flight, so I would pick up the car and wait for her in Austin. We would both ride to Killeen from there, about an hour and half away from the airport, but would make it before the day was up.

The plans were made, I picked up my tickets, and went to pick up Sis. We started early in the morning so we would still be there before the doctor left from the hospital. We arrived at the airport praising God for all that had transpired that day. We were speaking angels to take us the rest of the way through the day. Just as we walked into the terminal an Officer came directly to us and asked if he could help us!

We looked at each other and whispered, "Angels Unaware," and told him that would be great!

I was thinking we are middle aged women that really don't look like something men would be looking at, if you know what I mean. If they were looking to help someone it would be a cute little thing, certainly not us. That confirmed it even more that God had sent this angel in the form of this man in uniform to help us just as we had asked.

He seemed to know where we were going though we hadn't told him anything. As he guided us to the departure sight, we observed the departure list started showing everything

CANCELLED! There was a storm brewing outside like none I'd ever seen. Sis's flight was still on time in a couple hours but mine was cancelled. The Officer (angel) told us not to worry. He told us airlines worked with each other and though the public was not generally informed of it, they would honor my ticket through another airline provider. He opened a door that I never remembered seeing before, and walked us down this long corridor.

It seemed we had walked a long way and I have to admit we were starting to feel a bit silly for trusting this stranger (angel) to take us down a long hall that no one else was in. There were no other doors into this hallway either. Finally, there was an opening into a small area where a few people were working behind a desk. The Officer (angel) informed us that they would take care of us and it would be alright. We both turned to glance at the small line of people we were to wait behind, looked at each other, and then turned back to thank our guide. HE WAS GONE! THERE WAS NO WHERE HE COULD HAVE GONE!

We asked the people in line, "Where did that Officer go?" They acted like we were crazy.

"No seriously did you see where he went, we wanted to thank him again."

Everyone told us they didn't see anyone walk in with us let alone an Officer. Everyone notices an Officer as a person of authority, but no one in the line had seen this Officer.

Our turn came and both Sis and I told the gentleman behind the desk what the Officer had told us. He looked at us like we had lost our minds, but we knew for sure that he was an angel sent by God and what he said was the truth! We repeated what the Officer (angel) told us of how one airline was owned by another and they would be able to help us get to Killeen, Texas. The young man tried to tell us he was not able to do that, but he could see we were not going to take "no" for an answer. A young lady who identified herself as a manager stepped up asking how we had found them. We went through the whole spiel about how the Officer had taken us down the corridor and how he'd said they would help.

The manager said she had never heard of anything like that and she didn't think she could do anything to assist, but she would look into it. She sat down at the desk and started to work on the computer. Suddenly her mouth dropped opened.

"I have never seen anything like that!" she said as everyone behind her huddled up staring at the computer.

Finally, she told us she guessed she could help us! She would get us on the same flight and return flight with no extra charge. Sis and I always wondered what was on the computer screen that day that made the manager's mouth drop open and everyone behind her stare at the screen in amazement. I'm sure it changed her life that day, it certainly did our lives.

We thanked her and told her we were The Faith Sisters and we would say a prayer for her and called her by the name tag on her jacket. She quickly informed us that she had borrowed the jacket from someone else. She gave us her correct name and asked us to prayer for her. We agreed and said a prayer over her. We went back out the door we had come in through, but when we turned to go down the hall it wasn't there. The door led directly into the terminal. Sis and I rejoiced over the miracles and gifts shown to us that morning, and thanked God for sending Officer Angel.

Our travels, however, were not over with for the day. We both boarded the plane for Texas. As we rose above the clouds, I have never seen anything like it. Sis and I talked about how satan was trying hard to keep us from taking this trip safely because as we looked out the window of the plane it was like a giant storm was forming like one you would see out over the ocean. The billows of dark clouds rolled violently over each other like a giant swell off the ocean. It almost took our breath away. The darkness took on a life of its own, trying to wipe out everything in its path. It was an eerie feeling and we knew we had been spared by the hand of God.

We arrived in Austin two hours later than we were scheduled which created a problem with the car rental. Sis and I prayed about it and asked for more angels to make a way and solve this issue. The young lady checked to see what she could do to help and returned with an upgrade at no additional cost! Once again we praised God and thanked Him for the angels He'd sent before us as we drove off to the hospital in a better car than we had anticipated.

Arriving at the hospital we went directly to find Mother and found her in intensive care. She had tubes running everywhere, all sorts of IV's hooked up to her, and looked very frightened. We had been to Killeen a couple months previously at the care facility she was living in for Mother's Day surprising her with a concert. Mom did not seem surprised to see us together at the hospital, but it was obvious there was something seriously wrong.

We talked to her a few minutes and told her she would be fine and we would be right back to see her. As we walked out of the room, Sis and I looked at each other and agreed she was obviously not taking her bipolar and multiple personality syndrome medication. We had seen this personality before. She was thinking she was a small child, sitting there sucking her fingers with fear. We went directly to the doctor's office knowing exactly what we needed to ask for. He was a bit startled to see the look on our faces when we told him we knew he had not taken the time to read her records before treating Mother. We expressed in no uncertain terms that we expected her to be taken out of the ICU and placed in a regular room before we returned from the care facility with her glasses so she could see.

In my book, "On Fire for God," I explained that my mother was what is called bipolar and had multiple personalities. She had to stay on the medication to keep her in some state of normalcy. We had always given her the medication and told her it was for her heart because otherwise she would refuse to take the medications. It was not safe to be around her without them. When we had arrived at the hospital, we knew immediately what was going on. It is such a sad thing to see your mother as a three year old, sucking her fingers, and talking like a small child.

The care center had not caught that mother needed her meds either. They told us that they'd had to remove her roommate because mother was starting to scare the other woman. We picked up her glasses and informed them of the situation. We had talked to the doctor and he would be changing her meds. We explained they would need to tell mother the pills were for her heart. They agreed and told us how much they enjoyed her when she first came, adding they should have caught it when her moods had changed so drastically.

When we returned to the hospital, Mother had been moved to a regular room with no tubes, but she was still the small child and looking very devious. My brother and his boys arrived and brought her a hamburger and fries which were certainly not on her diet for dialysis, but no one had the heart to take them away from her. She looked so happy eating her burger and fries, acting like she had got away with something. We informed our brother about Mother's meds which he apparently was totally unaware of since he was too young to remember all the things that had happened. Maybe he was trying to forget like all of us wished we could.

Seeing things were under control and with the evening getting late, Sis and I were getting a bit tired so off to the hotel we went. I had found a hotel that was very reasonable and was easy to find. We grabbed a bit to eat, read our Bibles, and talked about the miraculous day we'd had. That night we slept soundly and woke in the morning feeling refreshed. We noticed there were several police cars at one end of the hotel parking lot, but when I asked Sis if she had heard anything she told me she slept like a baby. We shrugged our shoulders and headed to our brother's before going to the hospital.

He asked where we stayed and when we informed him of the name of the hotel his mouth dropped open. He told us that was a terrible part of town and there was a shooting and several people were killed there that previous night while we slept. Sis and I started laughing, but he didn't think it was humorous. We told him we'd had angels protecting us all the way there and expected them to take us home the same way.

We only spent a couple days in Killeen making sure Mother was doing okay. Another bruise in satan's eye happened when we headed out of Killeen. We spotted a Christian store going out of business and all the sound tracks were on sale for eighty percent off. Sis and I decided the Holy Ghost touched us as we picked them up to listen to on our drive back to the airport. That is how we started with most of our music and we actually learned a new song, "You've Gotta' Walk," on the way home from Killeen to Austin. The flight from Austin to Denver and then back to Phoenix was an uneventful one and we were happy to just share time with each other.

My sister had always been my best friend and I miss her so since she has now gone on to be with the Lord. I thank God for the time we had together and I know I will see her when I join her in heaven.

Many times I think we miss the angels that God has sent. We think we can do it on our own and that is not so. Let's not bore the angels God has sent to minister to us by giving them nothing to do. I pray you glean for what God has promised and ask Him to send the angels out to help guide and protect you.

I always ask for Warring Angels to come and protect us as we travel in the car. I know it has kept us from harm's way many times. I remember one incident as we were traveling up the mountain to the Joshua Room. It was raining so hard that day that part of the mountain had washed down blocking the road. We had to stop and turn around to take a different route.

We were running later than we had hoped, but I told Flo, my girlfriend that travels with me, that God was probably keeping us out of an accident. We found out later that some of the rocks that had fallen off the mountain had struck some automobiles along that road. If we had been on time we would have been there where the rocks came down. Thank You Father for sending Your protecting angels!

For He will give His angels [especial] charge over you to accompany and defend and preserve you in all your ways [of obedience and service]. (Psalm 91:11 AMP)

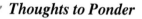

Thoughts to Ponder

Are not the angels all ministering spirits (servants) sent out in the service [of God for the assistance] of those who are to inherit salvation? (Hebrews 1:14 AMP)

Do not forget to show hospitality to strangers, for by so doing some people have shown hospitality to angels without knowing it. (Hebrews 13:2 NIV)

Father God has many ways He shows His love for us. One way is to send His angels to go before us, clear our paths, and protect us from the attacks of the enemy. However, as with every gift, that gift is useless unless it is used by the receiver of the gift. Left in the box and unused on the shelf, it cannot serve its purpose.

God expects you to use the gifts He has for you. Make it your daily practice to call upon the angels God has sent for you to use. You will be amazed at the peace and freedom you will feel as you call upon His angels to go before you no matter what your task or challenge.

Pray: *Father God, thank You for Your ministering angels. Thank You for the many gifts You have given me. Help me to remember to use and appreciate each and every one of those amazing gifts!*

CONCLUSION: WATCH FOR ANGELS

I know angels are there to protect us, and to give us messages from God. I hope I have inspired you to research where angels touched people's lives in the Bible. They are in the Bible to remind us of how God has not changed from the past to present.

We need to watch what we speak. If we can agree with something positive and make it happen, we can also agree with the negative and make that happen. We live in a voice activated world. God spoke things into order and we are made in His likeness. Your words create your future; let me inspire you to speak blessings into your life. Choose to speak words of comfort not despair, laughter not tears, joy not sadness, and life not death.

Watch for the angels in your life; we walk among them daily. Be blessed by God's provision for He has placed the angels to guide and keep you safe through the trials in your life.

God is 100% for your success. Whatever He has called you to do, He has made available to you everything you will need to accomplish it. Be aware, watch for divine opportunities and divine appointments as you go through your day. God loves you with an unconditional, everlasting love. Don't waste even one day by missing out on all that your loving Heavenly Father has available for you!

His divine power has given us everything we need for a godly life through our knowledge of him who called us by his own glory and goodness. Through these he has given us his very great and precious promises, so that through them you may participate in the divine nature, having escaped the corruption in the world caused by evil desires.

For this very reason, make every effort to add to your faith goodness; and to goodness, knowledge; and to knowledge, self-control; and to self-control, perseverance; and to perseverance, godliness; and to godliness, mutual affection; and to mutual affection, love. For if you possess these qualities in increasing measure, they will keep you from being ineffective and unproductive in your knowledge of our Lord Jesus Christ. But whoever does not have them is nearsighted and blind, forgetting that they have been cleansed from their past sins.

Therefore, my brothers and sisters, make every effort to confirm your calling and election. For if you do these things, you will never stumble, and you will receive a rich welcome into the eternal kingdom of our Lord and Savior Jesus Christ. (2 Peter 1:3-11 NIV)

ABOUT THE AUTHOR

Please check out The Faith Sisters, Inc. at: www.thefaith-sisters.com
Pay Pal is available for product purchases, albums, my sister's book, t-shirts, etc.
Donations may be made to The Faith Sisters, Inc. at this site also.
Contact us at: thefaithsisters@yahoo.com

Other books by Mary J. Wagner

"On Fire for God" is a book about faith in God through severe burns when I was eight years old and how my miraculous healing over time brought me into a wonderful relationship with our Lord and Savior, Jesus Christ. My two times to heaven have given me the vision of how important it is to share my life.

This is a story of many challenges in life and how the Lord sends the angels, Holy Spirit, and people to help us through our walk while here on this earthly plain. This book will be one you will want to share with someone you love. I will warn you this book is hard to get back in your hands after lending it out because it is a book that everyone wants to share because it is one of hope, faith, and God's grace.

"On Fire for God" can be purchased online, through your Kindle, Nook, and notebooks. This book can also be found through Barnes and Noble Book Stores and The Faith Sisters web site.

Thinking of writing your own book?

You can contact my friend and editor, Pamela McLaughlin at YourWrittenWord@yahoo.com. She will be glad to explain the process and help you accomplish your God-given goal of sharing your own story just as she helped me.

SMALL GROUP FACILITATOR'S GUIDE

Introduction: We Walk Among Angels

Introduce your small group to the author of this book by reading her brief testimony in the Preface of this book. You might also suggest they read the author's full story in her book, "On Fire for God." It would be great to have a copy of the book on hand for your group to look at. Ordering information is included at the end of this book.

Read or have members of your group, read out loud the Introduction to the book.

On many occasions in the Bible it tells of where people came in contact with and spoke to the angels. Ask your group if they remember any Bible stories where people came in direct contact with angels. (Examples from the New Testament might be the Mary and her husband-to-be Joseph who were both spoken to by an angel about the upcoming birth of Jesus.)

Read and discuss Psalm 8:5 where the Bible speaks of man and says God has made man a little lower than the angels.

Read the story of Elisha in 2 Kings 6:1-16 and then discuss 2 Kings 6:17.

And Elisha prayed, and said, "LORD, I pray thee, open his eyes, that he may see." And the LORD opened the eyes of the young man; and he saw: and, behold, the mountain was full of horses and chariots of fire round about Elisha.

Pray with your group and ask God to open their eyes to see as Elisha prayed for his servant in their time of need. *"Lord, I pray you open our eyes that we might see the work of Your ministering angels all around us daily."*

Suggest the members of the group begin keeping a journal of experiences where they feel God has sent His angels to them this week and to bring it with them next week. Tell them you would like to have them give their testimonies at your next gathering.

Ask your group to read chapter one titled "Protecting Angels" before you gather again for your next meeting.

Chapter 1: Protecting Angels

Begin your meeting by having some of your members share experiences they have recorded in their journals concerning angels from the previous week.

You may want to start the sharing time yourself to put your members at ease if they have not shared testimonies publically before.

Close this sharing time by thanking God for each of the testimonies of the previous week.

Read or have someone in your group read Psalm 91:11-12 in the King James Version of the Bible:

For he shall give his angels charge over thee, to keep thee in all thy ways. They shall bear thee up in their hands, lest thou dash thy foot against a stone.

Also read this verse in the Amplified translation to add meaning to what God has promised His angels will be sent to do for us.

For He will give His angels [especial] charge over you to accompany and defend and preserve you in all your ways [of obedience and service]. They shall bear you up on their hands, lest you dash your foot against a stone.

Discuss the things promised in this verse:
1- God has given His angels charge over us to defend us.
2- His angels are to keep us in His ways of obedience and service.
3- His angels are to bear us up or hold us up in their hands.
4- His angels are to keep us from stumbling over the obstacles along our paths to doing what He has called us to do.

Read or have someone from your group read Hebrews 1:14:

Are not the angels all ministering spirits (servants) sent out in the service [of God for the assistance] of those who are to inherit salvation? (AMP)

There were some questions asked at the beginning of Chapter 1 that you can ask your group now that they have read the stories of God's Protecting angels:

Have you ever awakened from a sound sleep and knew someone called your name out urgently?
Who did you think was calling you?
How many times have you thought, just for a moment, something could happen if you didn't move that broom, shovel, box, etc.?

How many times does something happen simply because we ignore that still voice we think we hear?

Read Proverbs 18:21 and then discuss how important it is to choose wisely the words we use.

Death and life are in the power of the tongue: and they that love it shall eat the fruit thereof.

Remind your group to continue recording in their journals as they see the work of God in their lives this upcoming week. Ask them to read Chapter Two before you gather together again next time.

Pray for your group: *Lord God, please send Your ministering angels to defend, protect and guard me, my family, my church, and all those who serve and worship You. Please help us to listen and heed Your still small voice. Teach us, Lord, how to be more aware of the words we use and how to choose our words more wisely. Thank You for Your angels and Your Holy Spirit.*

Chapter 2: Fire in the Hallway

Begin your meeting by having some of your members share experiences they have recorded in their journals concerning dreams or visions from the previous week.

Close this sharing time by thanking God for each of the testimonies of the previous week.

Most people don't want to think or talk about what they feel others would consider "not normal."

Ask your group if they have ever shared their dreams or visions with others and what kind of reaction they normally get from these people.

Discuss the idea that for Christians, receiving dreams and visions from God is normal.

Have your group read from the following list of examples in the Bible where God gave His children dreams and visions to warn them or prepare them for what was going to happen.

In Genesis 37:5-10 we read about the dreams Joseph had.

What happened when Joseph told his brothers and father about his dreams?

Suggest for further study they may want read the rest of the story about Joseph and his dreams and see how they came true.

In Matthew 2:13, 19-23 we read how God warned Joseph to protect Jesus from Herod and Archelaus.

Remind them Joseph also had a visit from an angel concerning the birth of Jesus. Joseph had already learned the importance of taking these dreams and visions seriously. What might have happened had he not done so?

The Bible says God never changes. He is the same yesterday, today, and forever (Hebrews 13:8).

Discuss what that means to us today concerning dreams and visions.

Discuss what we should do when we have a dream or a vision. For example: Pray for these situations whether for protection or wisdom in preparing for what God is telling us what is to come.

Remind your group to continue recording in their journals as they see the work of God in their lives this upcoming week. Ask them to read chapter three before your next group meeting.

Pray for your group: *Thank You Heavenly Father for sending us dreams and visions to warn and protect us, and to prepare us for what is to come. Help us to tune in and realize the importance of these dreams and visions, and teach us how to pray in accordance with what You are showing us. Thank You that You never change and that You are the same today, tomorrow, and forever.*

Chapter 3: Crazy Trip with Shrink

Begin your meeting by having some of your members share experiences they have recorded in their journals concerning the ways God sends people or angels to help them reassess where they are on life's path.

Close this sharing time by thanking God for each of the testimonies of the previous week.

Chapter three closed by asking us some very probing questions. It is uncomfortable to face these questions but important that we do.

Are you hiding behind something such as work, children, drugs, or alcohol?

Did any of you discover other things we can hide behind to keep us from having to face life's issues?

Did you discover you had been placing these things in your life instead of going to the Lord with the issues you need to face and deal with in your life?

What are some of the ways you have discovered to give God the opportunity to speak to you?

Read Psalm 34:17-19. What is the promise we are given in these verses?

Read 2 Corinthians 1:3-5.

Nothing compares to the relationship you can have with your loving Heavenly Father!

Remind your group to continue recording in their journals as they see the work of God in their lives this upcoming week. Ask them to read chapter four before your next group meeting.

Pray for your group using the scriptures you have read in your meeting: *Thank You Father God that You are the Father of mercies and the God of all comfort. Thank You for sending us Your comforting representatives in our time of need. Help us to receive them as a gift from You. Then show us how we can become one of Your comforters to others in their time of need.*

Chapter 4: Angels Take Time

Begin your meeting by having some of your members share experiences they have recorded in their journals concerning the ways God has answered their prayers.

Close this sharing time by thanking God for each of the testimonies of the previous week.

Read Matthew 18:18-19 in King James Version and then in the Amplified Translation for added insight into this passage of scripture spoken by Jesus to His disciples.

Verily I say unto you, whatsoever ye shall bind on earth shall be bound in heaven; and whatsoever ye shall loose on earth shall be loosed in heaven. Again I say unto you, that if two of you shall agree on earth as touching anything that they shall ask, it shall be done for them of my Father which is in heaven. (KJV)

Truly I tell you, whatever you forbid and declare to be improper and unlawful on earth must be what is already forbidden in heaven, and whatever you permit and declare proper and lawful on earth must be what is already permitted in heaven.

Again I tell you, if two of you on earth agree (harmonize together, make a symphony together) about whatever [anything and everything] they may ask, it will come to pass and be done for them by My Father in heaven. (AMP)

There are two important parts to Jesus' teaching.

1. When we bind or loose something on the earth as it says in the KJV, what does the Amplified version say this means we are doing?

2. What did Jesus say was one way of getting our prayers answered?

How does the Amplified translation define agreement?

What percentage of our prayers will be answered if we follow the instructions Jesus gave us in this scripture?

Read Daniel 10:2, 12-13.

In those days I Daniel was mourning three full weeks….Then said he said unto me, fear not, Daniel: for from the first day that thou didst set thine heart to understand and to chasten thyself before thy God, thy works were heard, and I am come for thy words. But the prince of the kingdom of Persia withstood me one and twenty days but, lo, Michael, one of the chief princes came to help me; and I remained there with the kings of Persian. (Daniel 10:2, 12-13)

How does this story of Daniel encourage us when it comes to waiting for God to answer our prayers?

Remind your group to continue recording in their journals as they see the work of God in their lives this upcoming week. Ask them to read chapter five before your next group meeting.

Pray for your group: *Thank You Father that You always hear our prayers and that You will send Your ministering angels to do Your bidding. We thank You that we can live with the assurance that Your will shall be done on earth as it is in heaven. Help us to seek to partner with You in seeing Your will come to pass as we pray individually and together with other members of Your Kingdom.*

Let's read the Lord's Prayer together:

Our Father which art in heaven, Hallowed be thy name.

Thy kingdom come, Thy will be done in earth, as it is in heaven.

Give us this day our daily bread.

And forgive us our debts, as we forgive our debtors.

And lead us not into temptation, but deliver us from evil: For thine is the kingdom, and the power, and the glory, for ever. Amen. (Matthew 6:19-13)

Chapter 5: Guide Me Holy Spirit

Begin your meeting by having some of your members share experiences they have recorded in their journals concerning the ways God communicated with them and the Holy Spirit comforted or led them this past week.

Close this sharing time by thanking God for each of the testimonies of the previous week.

Read John 14:26-27.

*But that **Comforter**, which is the **Holy Ghost**, whom the Father will send in my name, He shall teach you all things, and bring all things to your remembrance, whatsoever I have said unto you. Peace I leave with you, my peace I give unto you not as the world giveth, give I unto you. Let not your heart be troubled, neither let it be afraid.*

There are so many wonderful promises in this passage of scripture. Jesus also used it to describe the work of the Holy Spirit in our lives.

What are some of the things this passage says the Holy Spirit will do in our lives?

(Answers: teach all things, peace, comfort, do not have to be afraid)

Ask your group members if they have invited the Holy Spirit to be a part of their lives. If any of them would like to do so, encourage them to stay after and you will pray with them. It is important that you continue the class though and explain about speaking in tongues because many people immediately begin doing so when they invite the Holy Spirit into their lives.

Read 1 Corinthians 13:1.

Though I speak with the tongues of men and of angels...

What does "the tongues of men" mean in this scripture? (native language)

What does "the tongues of angels" refer to? (speaking in tongues)

In this chapter, God used the gift of speaking in tongues to do what?

We can all be used in the gifts of the Holy Spirit. We just have to be willing vessels. Make yourself available for God to use to minister to others no matter what gift the Holy Spirit works through you.

Read 1 Corinthians 12:7-11.

*But the manifestation of the Spirit is **given to each one for the profit of all**: for to one is given the **word of wisdom** through the Spirit, to another the **word of knowledge** through the same Spirit, to another **faith** by the same Spirit, to another **gifts of healings** by the* *same Spirit, to another the **working of miracles**, to another **prophecy**, to another **discerning of spirits**, to another **different kinds of tongues**, to another the **interpretation of tongues**. But one and the same Spirit works all these things, distributing to each one individually as He wills.* (NKJV emphasis added)

These gifts are mainly used to benefit whom? (others)
Who gives these gifts? (Holy Spirit)
Who is qualified to be used in the gifts of the Spirit? (everyone who is willing to be available to be used by God to bless others)

Encourage your group to learn more about these wonderful gifts of the Spirit. 1 Corinthians 12:1 says, "Now concerning spiritual *gifts*, brethren, I do not want you to be ignorant" (NKJV).

Read Mark 16:15-18.

*And He (Jesus) said to them, "**Go into all the world** and **preach the gospel** to every creature. He who believes and is baptized will be saved; but he who does not believe will be condemned. And these **signs will follow those who believe**: In My name they will **cast out demons**; they will **speak with new tongues**; they[1] will **take up serpents**; and if they drink anything deadly, it will by no means hurt them; they will **lay hands on the sick**, and they will recover."* (NKJV emphasis added)

As disciples of Jesus, what does this verse say Jesus expects us to do? (answers are in bold)

Read Mark 16:20 which tells us the disciples did go and do all of those things.

*And they went out and preached everywhere, the Lord working with them and confirming the word through the **accompanying signs**. Amen.* (NKJV emphasis added)

Remind your group to continue recording in their journals as they see the work of God in their lives this upcoming week. Ask them to read chapter six before your next group meeting.

Pray for your group using John 14:26-27 and Mark 16:15-20: *Thank You Heavenly Father for the gift of Your Holy Spirit. Thank You for sending us the Comforter who will guide us into all truth and direct our paths into safety. Thank You that You have equipped us through Your Holy Spirit to fulfill the great commission Jesus commanded us to fulfill during our lifetimes. Thank You that others will know You have sent us when these signs and wonders follow us every where You send us.*

Chapter 6: Blessed Friends

Begin your meeting by having some of your members share experiences they have recorded in their journals concerning the special friends God has sent into their lives. Ask them to share how the Holy Spirit led them to bless these special friends this past week.

Close this sharing time by thanking God for each of the testimonies of the previous week.

The Bible shows how important God says friends are in our lives. Read the following scriptures and discuss the impact of friends in your lives.

Proverbs 17:17 says, "A friend loves at all times, and a brother is born for adversity" (NKJV).

Ask if anyone has a friend that exemplifies this scripture.

Proverbs 18:24 says, "A man *who has* friends must himself be friendly,

But there is a friend *who* sticks closer than a brother" (NKJV).

How can we be a friend to our friends? Ask for examples.

Who is the friend that sticks closer than a brother?

In John 15:13 Jesus said, "Greater love has no one than this, than to lay down one's life for his friends" (NKJV).

Jesus not only made this declaration, He then did it. Discuss how He did it.

Close your meeting by reading this passage from the Message Bible. It is a beautiful message from Jesus.

"I've told you these things for a purpose: that my joy might be your joy, and your joy wholly mature. This is my command: Love one another the way I loved you. This is the very best way to love. Put your life on the line for your friends. You are my friends when you do the things I command you. I'm no longer calling you servants because servants don't understand what their master is thinking and planning. No, I've named you friends because I've let you in on everything I've heard from the Father." (John 15:11-15)

Remind your group to continue recording in their journals as they see the work of God in their lives this upcoming week. Ask them to read chapter seven before your next group meeting.

Pray for your group: *Father God, we desire to be the kind of friend Jesus is to us. Send Your Holy Spirit to guide us this week to be that friend that loves at all times, that is there for those in need, and stands by those who are suffering. Give us Your direction and wisdom that we can be there for those special friends*

*You have placed in our lives. Use us to be Your hands
and feet and to reflect Your heart this week. Help us
to answer You quickly and obediently every time Your
Holy Spirit calls.*

Chapter 7: God Rings

Begin your meeting by having some of your members
share experiences they have recorded in their journals concerning His still small voice guiding them the previous week.

Close this sharing time by thanking God for each of the
testimonies of the previous week.

Read 1 Kings 19:11-12.

There are many ways God can use to communicate with
His people. Ask your group for some examples from the Bible
of ways God used to guide and communicate with His people.

One example might be from the Old Testament when
God sent the cloud by day and the fire by night to guide the
children of Israel through the wilderness.

Another example from the New Testament is when Peter
had a vision of a great sheet coming out of heaven. When he
pondered what all this meant, the Holy Spirit gave him his
answer in Acts 10:19.

Take time to hear what wonderful things God has for you
when you draw near to Him. Allow the Holy Spirit to guide
you and His angels to work on your behalf.

Read 1 Corinthians 14:15 preferably in either the
Amplified or New Living Bible Translation as they will help
you explain the different ways of praying as guided by the
Holy Spirit.

*For if I pray in an [unknown] tongue, my spirit [by
the Holy Spirit within me] prays, but my mind is
unproductive [it bears no fruit and helps nobody].
Then what am I to do? I will pray with my spirit [by*

the Holy Spirit that is within me], but I will also pray [intelligently] with my mind and understanding; I will sing with my spirit [by the Holy Spirit that is within me], but I will sing [intelligently] with my mind and understanding also. (AMP)

For if I pray in tongues, my spirit is praying, but I don't understand what I am saying. Well then, what shall I do? I will pray in the spirit, and I will also pray in words I understand. I will sing in the spirit, and I will also sing in words I understand. (NLT)

This may give you an opportunity to pray with any members of your group that have not been filled with the Holy Spirit. Be open to the leading of the Holy Spirit as to His timing.

Remind your group to continue recording in their journals as they see the work of God in their lives this upcoming week. Ask them to read chapter eight before your next group meeting.

Pray for your group: *Father God, thank You for sending Your Holy Spirit to help guide us in all of Your ways. Help us to stay attuned to Your still small voice and be willing to be used by You to pray for those we may not even know. Thank You Father for helping those You direct to pray for us.*

Chapter 8: Complacency

Begin your meeting by having some of your members share experiences they have recorded in their journals concerning areas where God has shown them they have become complacent. Make sure they understand the meaning of complacency.

By transparently sharing what God has revealed to you this week, you will help the others to openly share what God has been showing them.

Close this sharing time by thanking God for each of the testimonies of the previous week.

Read Amos 6:1 in the NIV Translation of the Bible:

Woe to you who are complacent in Zion, and to you who feel secure on Mount Samaria, you notable men of the foremost nation, to whom the people of Israel come!

Also read Zephaniah 1:12 in the NIV Translation of the Bible:

At that time I will search Jerusalem with lamps and punish those who are **complacent***, who are like wine left on its dregs, who think, 'The Lord will do nothing, either good or bad.'*

Discuss why God will punish complacency.

What are some of the dangers of becoming complacent?

Remind your group to continue recording in their journals as they see the work of God in their lives this upcoming week. Ask them to read chapter nine before your next group meeting.

Pray for your group: *Father God, please search our hearts and reveal any areas where we may have become complacent. Our desire is to do Your will, as You require it, and in Your timing.*

Chapter 9: I'm Grateful

Begin your meeting by having some of your members share experiences they have recorded in their journals concerning opportunities they had this week to pay-it-forward. Remind them that pay-it-forward means we look for ways to show acts of kindness to those around us.

Be open to the Holy Spirit to reveal to you if there are members of your group that have never accepted God's free gift of love.

Close this sharing time by thanking God for each of the testimonies of the previous week and particularly for those who have accepted Jesus as their Lord and Savior.

Read Colossians 3:12-13.

Clothe yourselves therefore, as God's own chosen ones (His own picked representatives), [who are] purified and holy and well-beloved [by God Himself, by putting on behavior marked by] tenderhearted pity and mercy, kind feeling, a lowly opinion of yourselves, gentle ways, [and] patience [which is tireless and long-suffering, and has the power to endure whatever comes, with good temper]. Be gentle and forbearing with one another and, if one has a difference (a grievance or complaint) against another, readily pardoning each other; even as the Lord has [freely] forgiven you, so must you also [forgive]. (AMP)

Discuss what it means in the beginning of verse twelve when it says we are chosen and hand-picked by God to be His representatives.

Another verse that reflects this same idea is 2 Corinthians 5:20:

So we are Christ's ambassadors, God making His appeal as it were through us. We [as Christ's personal representatives] beg you for His sake to lay hold of the divine favor [now offered you] and be reconciled to God. (AMP)

Go over the list of traits listed in Colossians 3:12-13 that a true representative of God should exhibit to the world.

Note the end of verse thirteen where it tells us to "pay-it-forward." We are to extend forgiveness in the same measure God has forgiven us.

Remind your group to continue recording in their journals as they see the work of God in their lives this upcoming week. Ask them to read chapter ten before your next group meeting.

Pray for your group using the blessing from Numbers 6:24-26: *May the Lord bless you and watch, guard, and keep you. May He make His face to shine upon and enlighten you and be gracious, kind, merciful, and give favor to you. May the Lord lift up His approving countenance upon you and give you peace and tranquility of heart and life continually.*

Chapter 10: Hospital Apartment

Begin your meeting by having some of your members share experiences they have recorded in their journals concerning those that were a special blessing to them this week and those they were able to bless.

Close this sharing time by thanking God for each of the testimonies of the previous week.

Read the story of Dorcas in Acts 9:36-41.

What were some of the words the scriptures used to describe this lady? (i.e. always doing good, always helping the poor, made clothes for those in need)

What happened when this kind and generous woman became sick and died?

Why did the people of her neighborhood go to such extremes after she died?

Ask your group to really be alert and sensitive to the needs of those around them.

Remind your group to continue recording in their journals as they see the work of God in their lives this upcoming week. Ask them to read chapter eleven before your next group meeting.

Pray for your group: *Father God, give each of us Your eyes that we might see the hurting all around us, give us Your heart to want to help them, give us Your words that we might comfort them, and give us Your hands that we might be used by You in their lives.*

Chapter 11: Michelle Annie

Begin your meeting by having some of your members share what they have recorded in their journals concerning their experiences listening for and obeying God's promptings to sow into other's lives.

Close this sharing time by thanking God for each of the testimonies of the previous week.

Read 1 Corinthians 2:14.

But the natural man receiveth not the things of the Spirit of God: for they are foolishness unto him: neither can he know them, because they are spiritually discerned. (1 Corinthians 2:14)

Use the story of how God directed Gideon to defeat the Midianites in Judges 7 to help explain this biblical principle.

What were some of things God told Gideon to do that sounded like foolishness to the natural man?

What happened when Gideon did as God instructed him even though it seemed foolish at the time?

Ask if anyone has an example of this from their own lives. Share an example from your own life.

Remind your group that in the natural we have to be quiet enough in our lives to hear what the Lord is trying to tell us. We can't afford to miss this gift of the Holy Spirit that we are given when we accept Christ Jesus as our Lord. The Lord can help us out of trouble if we are willing to listen and have faith.

Read Psalm 37:3-9.

Discuss the awesome list of promises God gives us in these verse:

1- Trust God and enjoy safety.
2- Delight in God and He will give you the desires of your heart.
3- Commit to and trust in God and He will exalt your righteousness.
4- Be still and wait patiently and the Lord will handle the evil around you.
5- Hope in the Lord and you will inherit the land.

Remind your group to continue recording in their journals as they see the work of God in their lives this upcoming week. Ask them to read chapter twelve before your next group meeting.

Pray for your group using Psalm 37: *Thank You Heavenly Father that You continually send the Holy Spirit to teach and guide us in Your ways. Help us to listen more carefully, trust more readily, and obey more quickly so that we accomplish Your purposes each and every day. Thank You for Your promises to us as we trust and obey. Thank You for your promise to give us the desires of our hearts as we place our hope in You.*

Chapter 12: Speaking Blessings

Begin your meeting by having some of your members share experiences they have recorded in their journals concerning the ways they have seen God respond to their prayers and spoken blessings this past week. Especially ask them to share examples where their thoughts and intentions for other people seem to be sent out in the universe even though they are not spoken or how they were affected by the thoughts of others.

Close this sharing time by thanking God for each of the testimonies of the previous week and for sending His ministering angels in response to each of their prayers.

Discuss examples in the Bible where fathers prayed a blessing over their children.

Isaac blessed his son Jacob in Genesis 27:27-29.

What were Isaac's blessings over Jacob?

Jacob spoke blessings over Joseph's sons in Genesis 48:3-7.

What were the blessings given to these boys in verses 15-16?

Jacob spoke blessings over his son Joseph in Genesis 49:22-26.

What does Jacob declare over Joseph in verse 22?

Suggest they each write out a letter of blessings they would like to speak over their children or their grandchildren. Encourage them to bring their children (grandchildren) to them. If they are where they cannot personally put their hands on them, suggest they call them and read the letter of blessings they have written over them.

If they do have grandchildren, encourage them to share this lesson with their grown children so that they too can speak blessings over their own children and pass this biblical principle on to the next generation.

We are commanded by God to leave an inheritance, a legacy to our children and our grandchildren. What better legacy can we pass on to our children and grandchildren then that of God's blessing and favor spoken directly over their lives?

> *A good man leaves an inheritance [of moral stability and goodness] to his children's children, and the wealth of the sinner [finds its way eventually] into the hands of the righteous, for whom it was laid up.* (Proverbs 13:22 AMP)

Remind your group to continue recording in their journals as they see the work of God in their lives this upcoming week. Ask them to read chapter thirteen before your next group meeting.

> Pray for your group using Psalm 34:7: *I pray that the angel of the Lord encamp around these who revere and worship You, Father God, and ask that You deliver them from harm. I pray You remind them to speak protection and blessing over their children and that You will answer these prayers above and beyond what they think.*

Chapter 13: Are We Like Grass?

Begin your meeting by having some of your members share experiences they have recorded in their journals concerning areas of fear they have had to deal with this past week.

Close this sharing time by thanking God for each of the testimonies of the previous week.

Read Isaiah 51:12-13.

> *I, even I, am He who comforts you. Who are you that you fear mortal men, the sons of men, who are but grass, that you forget the Lord your Maker, Who*

stretched out the heavens and laid the foundations of the earth, that you live in constant terror every day because of the wrath of the oppressor, who is bent on destruction? (Isaiah 51:12-13 NIV)

Ask your group to fill in the blanks as you review the points brought out in this scripture. (When you read the statements below, leave out the underlined words.)

1. God is telling us He is the one who **comforts** us.
2. Who do we really think we are to fear mortal men who are like **grass?**
3. God reminds us that if we are living in fear of man then we have **forgotten** our Maker and Lord.
4. God asked us why we would put our focus on someone who would like to **destroy** us instead of keeping our eyes on Him.
5. In Isaiah 51:16 it says, God has **covered** you with the shadow of His hand.
6. Ask them to tell you the acronym for F.E.A.R. = **False Evidence Appearing Real**
7. In Psalm 23 it says, "though I walk through the valley of the **shadow** of death" (NKJV). It **does not** say through the Valley of Death.
8. Shadows tend to make things appear **greater** than they are.
9. Does it make it easier to understand when the spirit of fear comes to you knowing it does not come from God?

Discuss why this difference is importance as we deal with fear in our lives.

Use some or all of the following scriptures in dealing with this issue of fear of man:

2 Timothy 1:7 says, "For God has not given us a spirit of fear, but of power and of love and of a sound mind" (NKJV).

Psalm 27:1 says, "The LORD *is* my light and my salvation; whom shall I fear? The LORD *is* the strength of my life; of whom shall I be afraid?" (NKJV)

Proverbs 29:25 says, "Fear of man will prove to be a snare, but whoever trusts in the LORD is kept safe" (NIV).

Remind your group to continue recording in their journals as they see the work of God in their lives this upcoming week. Ask them to read chapter fourteen before your next group meeting.

> Pray for your group using Psalm 27:1: *Thank You Lord that You are our light, our salvation and the strength of our lives, and that we do not have to fear man. Help us to remember that fear is really false evidence appearing real and that only what You say is the truth. Thank You Father for Your protection and Your comfort even when we walk through the valley of the shadow of death. We know that with You we have nothing to fear.*

Chapter 14: Pumpkin Seed

Begin your meeting by having some of your members share experiences they have recorded in their journals concerning how the revelation of God's love has helped them deal with their fears this week.

Close this sharing time by thanking God for each of the testimonies of the previous week.

Last meeting you dealt with the fear of man. This week you dealt with other fears that may have been present in your life. Jesus knew His disciples would face fear when He returned to Heaven after completing His mission here on the earth. Reading the words Jesus spoke to His disciples before He returned to Heaven and the prayers He spoke over them will reassure us as His disciples today of the Father's love for us as we too seek to complete our God-given purpose here on the earth.

Read John 14:23-27 where Jesus begins to prepare His disciples to continue in ministry after He is gone back to Heaven. Ask you group to fill in the blanks (underlined words).

Jesus said the Father would send us a Helper who is the **Holy Spirit.**

He also said He was leaving us His **peace.**

How did Jesus describe this peace? (see verse 27).

Read the prayer Jesus prayed over His disciples in John 17:1-26.

In verse 15, Jesus prayed, "I do not pray that You should take them out of the world, but that You should keep them from the **evil one**" (NKJV).

Remind your group of the Lord's Prayer and how Jesus taught us as His disciples to pray in Matthew 6:9-13. Discuss the things Jesus instructs to pray for.

1. God's kingdom to be on earth as it is in heaven.
2. Our daily bread.
3. Forgive us for our mistakes as we forgive others.
4. Help us resist temptation.
5. Deliver us from the evil one.

The last part of verse 13 tells us why we do not have to allow fear to dominate our lives.

"For Yours (God) is the **kingdom** and the **power** and the **glory** forever" (NKJV).

Remind your group to continue recording in their journals as they see the work of God in their lives this upcoming week. Ask them to read chapter fifteen before your next group meeting.

Have your group pray the Lord's Prayer together as you conclude your meeting.

Chapter 15: Pigeons

Begin your meeting by having some of your members share experiences they have recorded in their journals concerning ways God has shown them how much He cares for them this past week.

Close this sharing time by thanking God for each of the testimonies of the previous week.

Read what Jesus said in Matthew 10:29-31.

Discuss how valuable we are to God the Father.

Read Matthew 6:25-34 in the Amplified Translation.

Therefore I tell you, stop being perpetually uneasy (anxious and worried) about your life, what you shall eat or what you shall drink; or about your body, what you shall put on. Is not life greater [in quality] than food, and the body [far above and more excellent] than clothing?

Look at the birds of the air; they neither sow nor reap nor gather into barns, and yet your heavenly Father keeps feeding them. Are you not worth much more than they?

And who of you by worrying and being anxious can add one unit of measure (cubit) to his stature or to the span of his life?

And why should you be anxious about clothes? Consider the lilies of the field and learn thoroughly how they grow; they neither toil nor spin. Yet I tell you, even Solomon in all his magnificence (excellence, dignity, and grace) was not arrayed like one of these.

But if God so clothes the grass of the field, which today is alive and green and tomorrow is tossed into the furnace, will He not much more surely clothe you, O you of little faith?

Therefore do not worry and be anxious, saying, What are we going to have to eat? or, What are we going to have to drink? or, What are we going to have to wear? For the Gentiles (heathen) wish for and crave and diligently seek all these things, and your heavenly Father knows well that you need them all.

But seek (aim at and strive after) first of all His kingdom and His righteousness (His way of doing and being right), and then all these things taken together will be given you besides.

So do not worry or be anxious about tomorrow, for tomorrow will have worries and anxieties of its own. Sufficient for each day is its own trouble.

Discuss the concepts Jesus presents in this passage of scripture.

> Life is more than **food and clothing**.
> The Father feeds the birds and we are more **valuable.**
> **Worrying** does not add anything or any time to our lives.
> If God feeds the birds and clothes the fields, do we need to worry?
> Instead of worrying Jesus says we are to seek first:
> **God's kingdom**
> **God's righteousness** (His way of doing and being right)

When we do what these two things what does Jesus promise God the Father will do for us?

Everything we needed will be given to us.

Remind your group to continue recording in their journals as they see the work of God in their lives this upcoming week. Ask them to read chapter sixteen before your next group meeting.

Pray for your group using Matthew 6:33-34: *Thank You Father that You not only know our needs but desire to give us everything we could ever need. Help us to seek You, Your way of doing things, and to please You in all that we say and do.*

Note: If you are not already doing so, encourage your group members to bring their Bibles to each meeting. Especially next meeting they will need to have their Bibles for the interaction time.

Chapter 16: Unlikely Events

Begin your meeting by having some of your members share experiences they have recorded in their journals concerning unexpected events that happened in their lives recently. Perhaps ask them to share some of their answers to the questions posed in the Things to Ponder section.

What do you feel controls these unusual experiences in your life?
When unexplained things happen to you what is your response?
Do you look for the answers when you see unexplained blessings?

When was the last time you stepped out of the box to do
something out of the normal realm?
What gives you the ability to reach beyond yourself and
touch another's life?
What kind of circumstance of events does this set in order?
Do you ask for the angels to protect you daily?
Do you ask the Holy Spirit to lead you each and every day?

Close this sharing time by thanking God for each of the
testimonies of the previous week.
There is one more question posed by this story that we
need to discover the answer for.
How do we keep our eyes on the solution and not
the problem?
If we keep our eyes on the problem we will perish like the
people who came out of Egypt and were smitten by the serpents. Moses made the staff with the snake on it for the people
to keep their eyes on instead of their bites, and when they
kept their eyes on the staff they were healed in Numbers 21:9.
The Bible has given us another example of why we need
to do this in the story of Peter walking on the water; read
Matthew 14:22-31.

What happened when Peter took his eyes off of the solu-
tion and focused on the problem instead?
What was Peter's problem?
Who was Peter's solution?
What did Jesus say to Peter in verse 31?

Faith is an action word. When we step out and act in faith,
the Lord will show us the next step. It doesn't seem to appear
until the first step has been made in faith. Just as in the action
movies when the person cannot see where their next step will
be, but steps out anyway due to an undesirable effect of doom
behind them. They step out in faith and the footing is there

under their foot, even though it cannot be seen from their vantage point with the natural eyes.

We too must step out when prompted by the Lord. He will provide the way; He will never send us where He cannot reach us.

Read Proverbs 3:5-6.

What is God's promise in this passage of scripture?

Read Psalm 139:7-12.

Is there any place we can go that puts us out of His reach?

Trust God, He will not let us fall as long as we keep our eyes on Him and don't get swayed by our surroundings. We are to keep our eyes on the solution not the problem.

Remind your group to continue recording in their journals as they see the work of God in their lives this upcoming week. Ask them to read chapter seventeen before your next group meeting.

Pray for your group using Psalm 139: *Thank You Father God that there is no place we can go or no circumstance that can happen to us that You are not there with us. Help us to keep our eyes focused on You as our solution. Help us to speak the solution instead of the problem so that the world around us can see Your hand on our lives. May our lives be a witness of You even in those unlikely events that we come across.*

Chapter 17: Watch God's Hand

Begin your meeting by having some of your members share experiences they have recorded in their journals concerning the revelations they received from spending time reading God's Word, learning of His great love, and dealing with areas of hidden fear in their lives.

Close this sharing time by thanking God for each of the testimonies of the previous week.

Funny how fears try to hide just deep enough and far back enough that we almost think they are not really there.

Read 1 John 4:17-18 from the Message Bible:

God is love. When we take up permanent residence in a life of love, we live in God and God lives in us. This way, love has the run of the house, becomes at home and mature in us, so that we're free of worry on Judgment Day—our standing in the world is identical with Christ's. There is no room in love for fear. Well-formed love banishes fear. Since fear is crippling, a fearful life—fear of death, fear of judgment—is one not yet fully formed in love.

Discuss what it means for us to take up permanent residence in a life of love.

How do we allow God's love to "run our homes"?

How do we make our lives free of worry?

Read what Jesus said about worry in Matthew 6:24-25 in the Message Bible:

If you decide for God, living a life of God-worship, it follows that you don't fuss about what's on the table at mealtimes or whether the clothes in your closet are in fashion. There is far more to your life than the food you put in your stomach, more to your outer appearance than the clothes you hang on your body. Look at the birds, free and unfettered, not tied down to a job description, careless in the care of God. And you count far more to him than birds.

How does Jesus describe the Father's love for us?

It takes guts to bring those fears into the light and deal with the root of the evil that has had a hold on us. We do not need to accept the spirit of fear. We need to realize that it

is just a spirit sent from the evil one to keep us from being blessed by the Lord. We have every right to command that spirit of fear to go in the name of Jesus and it has to flee.
Read James 4:7.

Submit yourselves therefore to God. Resist the devil, and he will flee from you. (James 4:7)

So let God work his will in you. Yell a loud no to the Devil and watch him scamper. Say a quiet yes to God and he'll be there in no time. Quit dabbling in sin. Purify your inner life. Quit playing the field. Hit bottom, and cry your eyes out. The fun and games are over. Get serious, really serious. Get down on your knees before the Master; it's the only way you'll get on your feet. (James 4:7-10 The Message)

Remind your group to continue recording in their journals as they see the work of God in their lives this upcoming week. Ask them to read chapter eighteen before your next group meeting.

Pray for your group using James 4:7-10: *Help us Father God to let You work Your will in us. Remind us daily that we can yell a loud "no" to the devil and show us how he has to flee from us at the mention of Jesus' name. Help us to say a quiet "yes" to Your love and Your way.*

Chapter 18: Joy of the Word

Begin your meeting by having some of your members share experiences they have recorded in their journals concerning the revelations they received from spending time reading God's Word.

Close this sharing time by thanking God for each of the testimonies of the previous week.

Note: Because this week's lesson is about becoming regular in reading God's Word, have your members look up the scriptures in their own Bibles and perhaps have them read out of the various translations they are using. You will be helping them learn how to find their way through the Bible and giving them hands on training in searching the Scriptures for answers to life's issues.

Read 2 Timothy 3:16-17 (AMP) and discuss the benefits of studying the scriptures on a daily basis.

Every Scripture is God-breathed (given by His inspiration) and profitable for instruction, for reproof and conviction of sin, for correction of error and discipline in obedience, [and] for training in righteousness (in holy living, in conformity to God's will in thought, purpose, and action), so that the man of God may be complete and proficient, well fitted and thoroughly equipped for every good work.

Read Hebrews 4:12 (AMP).

For the Word that God speaks is alive and full of power [making it active, operative, energizing, and effective]; it is sharper than any two-edged sword, penetrating to the dividing line of the breath of life (soul) and [the immortal] spirit, and of joints and marrow [of the deepest parts of our nature], exposing and sifting and analyzing and judging the very thoughts and purposes of the heart.

Read Matthew 7:7-8.

Ask, and it shall be given you; seek, and ye shall find; knock, and it shall be opened unto you: For every one that asketh receiveth; and he that seeketh findeth; and to him that knocketh it shall be opened.

How many people does this scripture say can seek, knock, and find the door to our Heavenly Father opened to them?

What are the restrictions given by God?

Read Matthew 7:9-11. Discuss the importance of parents teaching their children about God and not leaving it all up to the Sunday School programs.

Or what man is there of you, whom if his son ask bread, will he give him a stone? Or if he ask a fish, will he give him a serpent? If ye then, being evil, know how to give good gifts unto your children, how much more shall your Father which is in heaven give good things to them that ask him?

Perhaps discuss ways to help your group members lead children to loving the Word of God and accepting Jesus Christ as their personal Lord and Savior.

Remind your group to continue recording in their journals as they see the work of God in their lives this upcoming week. Ask them to read chapter nineteen before your next group meeting.

Pray for your group using Hebrews 4:12: *Thank You Heavenly Father for Your Word that is alive and full of power that energizes our lives and gives us effective tools to handle whatever we face each and every day. We thank You that as we seek You, You will make Yourself available to us and give us Your wisdom and guidance for our daily lives.*

Chapter 19: God's Love Introverted

Begin your meeting by having some of your members share experiences they have recorded in their journals concerning the results they have experienced from the principle of sowing and reaping.

Close this sharing time by thanking God for each of the testimonies of the previous week.

Read Galatians 6:7-10. Discuss the key points of this passage of scripture as you have your group fill in the blanks.

1. Do not be deceived: God is not **mocked** (verse 7).
2. He who sows to the flesh will reap **corruption** (verse 8a).
3. He who sows to the Spirit will reap **everlasting life** (verse 8b)
4. Let us not grow weary in doing **good** (verse 9a).
5. For in due season we will **reap** if we do not lose heart (verse 9b).
6. Therefore, as we have the opportunity, let us do **good to all** (verse 10).

Read 2 Corinthians 9:6-8, and 10-11.

1. He who sows **sparingly** will reap **sparingly** (verse 6a).
2. He who sows **bountifully** will reap **bountifully** (verse 6b).
3. Let us give not **grudgingly** but **cheerfully** (verse 7).
4. All grace abounds toward you that you always have all **sufficiency** (verse 8a). Which means your resources will allow you to fulfill the rest of the verse.
5. And may have **abundance** for every good work (verse 8b).
6. Who supplies seed to the sower? (God) Is it good seed?

7. Who multiplies the seed? (God) Why does He multiply it?
8. Your generosity will bring forth **thanksgiving to God** (verse 11).

Read Philippians 4:8.

What are the things God tells us we should think on so that the harvest of our day will be God's peace and joy?

Remind your group to continue recording in their journals as they see the work of God in their lives this upcoming week. Ask them to read chapter twenty before your next group meeting.

Pray for your group using Psalm 19:14 and Philippians 4:8: *Let the words of our mouths, and the meditations of our hearts, be acceptable in Thy sight, O Lord. May our thoughts focus on what is true, right, pure, lovely, admirable, excellent, and praiseworthy so that Your peace reigns in our lives no matter what comes our way. Help us to sow good seed so that we can reap thanksgiving for You from those we sow into.*

Chapter 20: Straighten Up

Begin your meeting by having some of your members share experiences they have recorded in their journals concerning the results they have experienced from spending time with God every day.

Close this sharing time by thanking God for each of the testimonies of the previous week.

Ask them to define the word "gift" based on this chapter. Read Ephesians 2:8-9.

*For it is by grace you have been saved, through
faith—and this is not from yourselves, it is the gift of
God—not by works, so that no one can boast* (NIV).

What does this verse say is the gift of God? (salvation)
What do we have to do to "earn" this gift? (we
cannot earn it)
Can we receive this gift by the "works" that we do
for God? (no)
Why does God say He does not want us to try to earn this
gift through our works? (so we cannot boast)
Read John 1:17.

*For while the Law was given through Moses, grace
(unearned, undeserved favor and spiritual blessing)
and truth came through Jesus Christ.* (AMP)

If it is by grace that we are saved, how to we attain this
grace? (only through Jesus Christ)
Once Jesus has become our Lord and Savior, He offers
us a multitude of other free gifts.
In the story you read in this chapter, what gift did He give
to the author?
What did the author do to receive this gift?
Read Matthew 11:28-30.

*Come unto me, all ye that labour and are heavy laden,
and I will give you rest. Take my yoke upon you, and
learn of me: for I am meek and lowly in heart; and
ye shall find rest unto your souls. For my yoke is easy
and my burden is light.*

Ask your group if any of them have heavy burdens that
they need to allow Jesus to help them carry. Encourage them
to spend time with the Lord and allow Him to help them.

Remind your group to continue recording in their journals as they see the work of God in their lives this upcoming week. Ask them to read chapter twenty-one before your next group meeting.

Pray for your group using Ephesians 2:8-9 and Matthew 11:28-30. *Father God, we thank You for the wonderful gift of Your Son Jesus Christ. We know it is only through Your grace and Jesus' willing sacrifice that we have been able to receive this gift. We thank You for the promise of help with whatever burden we are facing in our lives no matter how big or small. Help us to turn to You and receive from You what we need every single day.*

Chapter 21: Time Flies By

Begin your meeting by having some of your members share experiences they have recorded in their journals concerning what God has revealed to them about the beauty all around them.

Close this sharing time by thanking God for each of the testimonies of the previous week.

Read the wisdom shared by King Solomon in these excerpts from Ecclesiastes 3:11-13.

He has made everything beautiful in its time...I know that nothing is better for them than to rejoice, and to do good in their lives...It is a gift of God. (NKJV)

Ask them to remember what it means to receive a gift from God.

There is an interesting story recorded in the Bible about two sisters named Martha and Mary that talks about their relationship with Jesus when He walked on this earth.

Martha had a wonderful servant's heart and wanted to make sure Jesus and His disciples were comfortable and well fed when they visited her home. Her sister Mary was so engrossed in the words of Jesus that she neglected some of her duties and ended up just sitting at His feet to listen.

Martha realized some of the preparations had not been completed and discovered Mary sitting at the feet of Jesus. The Bible records the interesting interchange between Martha and Jesus that then occurred.

But Martha was distracted with much serving, and she approached Him and said, "Lord, do You not care that my sister has left me to serve alone? Therefore tell her to help me."

And Jesus answered and said to her, "Martha, Martha, you are worried and troubled about many things. But one thing is needed, and Mary has chosen that good part, which will not be taken away from her." (NKJV)

Discuss what Jesus was telling Martha about being distracted by busyness, even if it is for the Lord.

Read again Psalm 118:24.

This is the day the LORD has made; We will rejoice and be glad in it.

Encourage everyone to take time to enjoy all that God has prepared for them each and every day.

Remind your group to continue recording in their journals as they see the work of God in their lives this upcoming week. Ask them to read chapter twenty-two before your next group meeting.

Pray for your group using Psalm 118:24: *Thank You, Father God for this beautiful world You have given us. Thank You for our families and friends. What precious gifts You have given us. Thank You that You have made each day especially for us. Remind us to rejoice and be glad in it. Remind us to share Your love with others even if it is only a smile accompanied by "God loves you!"*

Chapter 22: Are You Too Busy?

Begin your meeting by having some of your members share experiences they have recorded in their journals concerning what God has revealed to them about being too busy in their lives.

Close this sharing time by thanking God for each of the testimonies of the previous week.

There were some very pertinent questions asked at the beginning of this chapter that we should begin to be able to answer now that they have been brought to our attention by this lesson.

Who makes me so busy I don't get anything done?

Why am I so exhausted at the end of the day and still wonder what I have accomplished?

Am I willing to take the time to find out, spend time in the Word, and learn to hear the Lord's voice clearly?

Were we able to start dealing with these questions this week?

Read 2 Timothy 1:7.

What does this tell us about our minds?

Read 1 John 4:4.

What does this verse tell us about our ability to take control of our lives and overcome the busyness the world tries to overwhelm us with?

Read Psalm 46:10.

What does this verse say is the answer to knowing what to do and how to access the very best God has for us?

One more question must be answered: How do we stop this vicious cycle of busyness in our lives?

Read 2 Peter 1:3-4.

What does this passage tell us God has given us to overcome the temptation to become too busy and avoid being drawn away from God's plan for our lives?

Remind your group to continue recording in their journals as they see the work of God in their lives this upcoming week. Ask them to read chapter twenty-three before your next group meeting.

Pray for your group using 2 Timothy 1:7, 1 John 4:4, and Psalm 46:10: *Thank You, Heavenly Father that You have not given us the spirit of fear but of a sound mind. Thank You for Your Holy Spirit who reminds us daily that greater is He that is in us than he who is in the world. Help us Father, to set aside time every day to be still and get to know You better, and to know Your plan for our lives so that we can truly achieve and access Your very best for us.*

Chapter 23: Boundaries

Begin your meeting by having some of your members share experiences they have recorded in their journals concerning the results they have seen from following the life changing guides given in this lesson.

Close this sharing time by thanking God for each of the testimonies of the previous week.

Last week we talked about the fact God has equipped us to escape the distractions of the world in 2 Peter 1:3-4. Let's read the rest of that passage for even more insight as to how to implement all that God has given us in our lives to bring order instead of disorder, peace instead of frustration, and productivity instead of unfruitfulness.

Read 2 Peter 1:5-10 then discuss the list and the benefits given in this passage.

God gave us a progressive list in this passage which means they are steps to reach the desired outcome or goal:

    a.   Add to your faith **goodness or virtue**
    b.   Add to your goodness **knowledge**
    c.   Add to your knowledge **self-control**
    d.   Add to your self-control **perseverance**
    e.   Add to your perseverance **godliness**
    f.   Add to your godliness **brotherly kindness**
    g.   Add to you brotherly kindness **love**

Discuss ways to accomplish the above list.

At the end of this list God also gives us the benefits of doing the things on His list:

1. They will keep us from being **barren and unfruitful** which can also be translated as ineffective and unproductive

2. If we do these things we will never **stumble.** Notice God is saying we will *never* fall or stumble. That is quite a promise!

Remind your group to continue recording in their journals as they see the work of God in their lives this upcoming week. Ask them to read chapter twenty-four before your next group meeting.

Pray for your group using 1 Corinthians 14:33 as well as 2 Peter 1:5-10: *Thank You, Father God that You are a God of order and not disorder, a God of peace and not frustration or confusion. Help us to focus on the lists You have given us in Your Word like the one in 2 Peter that we studied today. We desire to be fruitful and effective in fulfilling what You have called us to do in our lives. Please give us Your guidance as we strive to use the gifts You have given effectively every day to serve You.*

Chapter 24: The Covenant of Marriage

Begin your meeting by having some of your members share experiences they have recorded in their journals concerning what they may have learned concerning their marriage relationship from reading this chapter on the covenant of marriage.

Close this sharing time by thanking God for each of the testimonies of the previous week.

Covenant is a word most people today do not understand. Many seem to think covenant and contract mean the same thing. Consider the following:

A Contract contains limited liability and often includes loopholes so if one party does not keep up their part of the bargain, the contract can be declared null and void.

Covenant on the other hand means unconditional or unlimited liability. The marriage covenant established by God was intended to last a life time.

The marriage vows we make on our wedding day are the promises we are making not only to our spouse, but to God of how we will handle this relationship and treat the gift of the spouse that He has given us.

Ask if they would share some of the vows they made to one another on their wedding day if they are already married.

For those not yet married, ask them what vows they would make and like to have their potential spouse make to them at their wedding.

There are two key scriptures that show that God is indeed a witness at our weddings and expects us to honor the vows we make to one another before Him.

Read Malachi 2:14 which is mainly directed at the man.

The LORD has been witness between you and the wife of your youth, with whom you have dealt treacherously; yet she is your companion and your wife by covenant. (NKJV)

Read Proverbs 2:17 which is mainly directed at the woman.

Who has left the partner of her youth and ignored the covenant she made before God. (NIV)

Discuss what is learned from these two verses.
Read Ecclesiastes 4:9-12.

Two are better than one, because they have a good reward for their labor. For if they fall, one will lift up his companion. But woe to him who is alone when he falls, for he has no one to help him up. Again, if two lie down together, they will keep warm; But how can one be warm alone? Though one may be overpowered by another, two can withstand him. And a threefold cord is not quickly broken. (NKJV)

Remind your group to continue recording in their journals as they see the work of God in their lives this upcoming week. Ask them to read chapter twenty-five before your next group meeting.

Pray: *Heavenly Father, remind us to pray for and be thankful for the spouse You have given us or the spouse You are going to give us. Remind us everyday what a wonderful gift You have given us. Remind us to never be too busy to spend quality time with our spouse. Show us how we can build each other up and become even stronger as we work together with You. Thank You that our threefold cord with You is not quickly or easily broken.*

Chapter 25: The Blessings of a Mom

Begin your meeting by having some of your members share experiences they have recorded in their journals concerning their relationships with their own mothers.

Close this sharing time by thanking God for each of the testimonies of the previous week.

Read Exodus 20:12.

God instructs us to honor our parents because then our days will be **long** in the land He has given us.

Discuss what this means if we obey.

What might the consequences be for disobeying this command?

Note: Our children will observe how we honor our parents and will honor us in the same way we model for them.

The author's Grandmother was a mentor for her all of her life.

Ask your group how they would define a mentor (i.e. adviser, counselor, guide, teacher).

What was one of the ways this grandmother mentored her granddaughter? (She would never give me the answer to a question, but would ask me a question that would make me find the answer for myself.)

There is an old adage that says, "You can give a person a fish but tomorrow he will be hungry and need another from you. But if you teach that person to fish, then he can provide for himself."

Read Matthew 4:19. Jesus told His disciples He was going to teach them to be fishers of men. Discuss what that means in light of understanding what it means to be a mentor.

We are called to be mentors to our grown natural children and any spiritual children God sends us.

Remind your group to continue recording in their journals as they see the work of God in their lives this upcoming week. Ask them to read chapter twenty-six before your next group meeting.

Pray for your group: *Heavenly Father, we are so thankful for Your love and care and for sending Jesus to be an example for us as to how to love and mentor our children. Give us wisdom as our children grow from childhood to adulthood that we might reflect Your love to them whatever stage in life we are at in their lives. Help us to honor our own parents and to be the godly parents You have called us to be.*

Chapter 26: God Brings Me a Mom

Begin your meeting by having some of your members share experiences they have recorded in their journals concerning the special people God has brought into their lives.

Close this sharing time by thanking God for each of the testimonies of the previous week.

Read Psalm 37:4 which says, "Delight thyself also in the LORD: and he shall give thee the desires of thine heart."

Ask for examples of how God has given them the desires of their hearts.

Read Psalm 27:10 which says, "Even if my father and mother abandon me, the LORD will hold me close" (NLT).

Many people think this scripture is just for those who are orphans but many children today experience lack of parental guidance even if their parents still live in the same home with them.

Ask if anyone in your group either experienced this type of "abandonment" or know of children who have.

Suggest ways God might use us to help fill those voids in the lives of these children like He sent MaMa B to the author.

Read Psalm 68:5 which says, "A father of the fatherless, a defender of widows, *is* God in His holy habitation" (NKJV).

Even though we have been talking about mothers in this section, the same can be said of fatherlessness in today's society. Many children are being raised in single parent homes for one reason or another.

Ask your group to think of ways to help those families in their churches or communities that are single-parent homes. Sometimes helping the single parent helps the child and gives that parent more time with their child.

Remind your group to continue recording in their journals as they see the work of God in their lives this upcoming week. Ask them to read chapter twenty-seven before your next group meeting.

Pray for your group: *Thank You, Father God that You are there for the widows and the fatherless or motherless no matter what the situation might be. Give*

*us eyes to see their needs and help us to listen for
Your guidance in helping these families and children
lead more productive and fulfilled lives. Thank You
for those You have sent into our lives to help "father
and mother" us.*

Chapter 27: Broken Pieces

Begin your meeting by having some of your members
share experiences they have recorded in their journals concerning times they feel God has had them on His potter's
wheel and in His kiln.

Close this sharing time by thanking God for each of the
testimonies of the previous week.

Read Isaiah 64:8. Discuss the different steps outlined in
this chapter in the making of the porcelain doll and compare
them to things God may do in our lives to refine us and make
us into His beautiful vessel.

1. Mix and pour the slip into the mold.
2. Patiently wait while the slip sets.
3. Gently remove it out of the mold.
4. Sand off the rough edges.
5. Place the pottery in the kiln.
6. Sand off the rough edges and polish.
7. Paint the vessel.
8. Place the painted vessel once again in the fire.

Read Joshua 1:5.

What is the amazing promise God has given us in this
scripture?

Read the story of Shadrach, Meshach, and Abednego
from Daniel 3.

Why were these Jewish men thrown into the fiery furnace?

Who does it say in verse 25 was in the fiery furnace with them?

What condition were they in when they were taken out of the fire?

What did the king decree because of the steadfastness of Shadrach, Meshach, and Abednego?

What does verse 30 say the king then did with the three Jewish men?

Remind your group to continue recording in their journals as they see the work of God in their lives this upcoming week. Ask them to read chapter twenty-eight before your next group meeting.

Pray for your group: *Thank You, Heavenly Father that You are the potter and we are the clay. Help us to remember that You are working to make us into a beautiful vessel of honor even when the process seems painful. Thank You for Your promise to be with us no matter where life takes us or the fiery tests and tribulations we may have to endure. Thank You for Your love and patience with us as You mold us into a vessel You can use in Your kingdom.*

Chapter 28: What Piece Are You?

Begin your meeting by having some of your members share experiences they have recorded in their journals concerning times they may have felt like they were not fitting into the puzzle of life or perhaps doubted God had a plan for them.

Close this sharing time by thanking God for each of the testimonies of the previous week.

This week is important to understand that God does not make junk. Neither did He mess up the mold when He created each one of us.

Read Psalm 139:13-16 in the New Living Translation.
*You made all the delicate, inner parts of my body and
knit me together in my mother's womb. Thank you for
making me so wonderfully complex! Your workmanship is marvelous—how well I know it. You watched
me as I was being formed in utter seclusion, as I was
woven together in the dark of the womb. You saw me
before I was born. Every day of my life was recorded
in your book. Every moment was laid out before a
single day had passed.*

Discuss how awesome it is to realize how God intricately
formed every part of each of our beings.
Read Jeremiah 29:11 in the New International Version.

*For I know the plans I have for you, declared the Lord,
plans to prosper you and not to harm you, plans to
give you hope and a future.* (Jeremiah 29:11 NIV)

Who would we rather have setting up the plans for our
lives, God or us?
Here is an interesting story that may shed some light on
why we need to leave the "steering" of our lives to God.
A family was traveling together on a beautiful old river
boat on the grand Mississippi River. They had been vaca-
tioning nearby and decided they could not go home without
riding one of these magnificent paddle wheel steam boats. It
was a beautiful warm day and the riverboat ride was sure to
be an exciting one. The scenery along the river was beautiful
until they rounded a sharp bend in the river. Suddenly they
were immersed in a cloud of very thick fog.
Startled, the family huddled together on the lower deck
clinging to the side rails and straining their eyes to try to catch
a glimpse of the shoreline. Fearful they were going to crash
into the shore, they asked a crew member if they needed to

don their life jackets. The crew member shook his head no as he explained that the captain knew exactly what he was doing and could safely guide them through the fog.

Seeing that the family was still not convinced, the wise crew member invited them to come and talk to the captain about their concerns. As they climbed the stairs to the captain's wheel house, they realized the captain was seated high above the foggy cloud that had surrounded them on the lower decks. He could clearly see the path in front of them and was indeed guiding them safely through the fog on target for their destination.

Read Isaiah 55:8.

For my thoughts are not your thoughts, neither are your ways my ways, saith the LORD.

Remind your group to continue recording in their journals as they see the work of God in their lives this upcoming week. Ask them to read chapter twenty-nine before your next group meeting.

Pray for your group using Psalm 139:13-16 in the New Living Translation. *Thank You, Heavenly Father that You made all the delicate, inner parts of our bodies and knit us together in our mother's womb. Thank You for making us so wonderfully complex! Your workmanship is marvelous—how well we know it. Thank You that You watched as we were being formed in utter seclusion and woven together in the dark of the womb. Thank You that every day of our lives was recorded in Your book and every moment was laid out before a single day had passed. Thank You for the awesome plans You have in place for each of us and the beautiful "puzzle" You are assembling with each of us as Your specially designed pieces.*

Chapter 29: Airlines and Angels

Begin your meeting by having some of your members share experiences they have recorded in their journals concerning experiences they have had with angels going before them and protecting them.

Close this sharing time by thanking God for each of the testimonies of the previous week.

Read Hebrews 1:14.

Are not all angels ministering spirits sent to serve those who will inherit salvation? (NIV)

Are not the angels all ministering spirits (servants) sent out in the service [of God for the assistance] of those who are to inherit salvation? (AMP)

Discuss the only requirement for calling upon these ministering angels (which is salvation through Jesus Christ).

Read Psalm 91:11.

For He will give His angels [especial] charge over you to accompany and defend and preserve you in all your ways [of obedience and service]. (AMP)

Emphasize the fact that God wants us to be able to accomplish the tasks He has set before us and will send His angels to assist us if we just ask.

Read Hebrews 13:2.

Do not forget to show hospitality to strangers, for by so doing some people have shown hospitality to angels without knowing it. (NIV)

Remind them to be aware that we walk among God's angels and to be thankful for God's provision.

Read the story of the angel God sent to free the Apostle Peter from prison in Acts 12:5-9.

Is anything too difficult for our God?

Pray for your group: *Thank You, Heavenly Father that nothing is too difficult for You. Thank You for Your ministering angels that are always there and ready to answer our needs. We are grateful for Your provision as we set about to accomplish what You have called us to do each and every day.*

CPSIA information can be obtained at www.ICGtesting.com
Printed in the USA
BVOW07s0017251013

334587BV00001B/1/P